For a
SHILLING
            a day

For a
SHILLING
a day

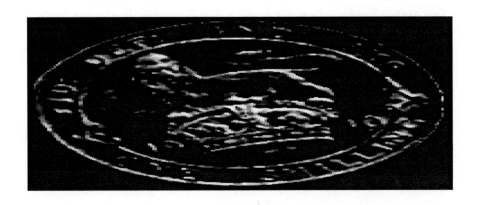

Peter Rhodes

BANK
HOUSE
BOOKS

First published in the United Kingdom in 2010 by

Bank House Books

PO Box 3

NEW ROMNEY

TN29 9AJ UK

www.bankhousebooks.com

British Library Cataloguing in Publication Data
A catalogue record for this book is available from the British Library

ISBN 9781904408642

Typesetting and origination by Bank House Books
Printed by Lightning Source

DEDICATION

To all the soldiers, sailors, airmen and civilians who have shared their
time and memories with me.

To the *Express & Star* for sending me to the Falklands, Sarajevo,
Vietnam and the Gulf and to the now-peaceful battlefields of two world
wars. To colleagues John Ogden and Mike Fox for help with a couple of
the Normandy interviews. To my wife, Sally, for endless help with the
proof-reading. And special thanks to George Jones, Reuben Welsh and
Alf Wilson, who on 6 June 1944 helped to save this planet from
madness. Thanks for their company, friendship and help as we walked
the course in Normandy, fifty years on.

CONTENTS

CONTENTS

FOREWORD

Journalism is the first draft of history and usually has a shorter shelf life than a loaf of bread. Every one of the interviews and dispatches in this book, conducted over the quarter-century between 1983 and 2008, deserves to survive a little longer and to reach a bigger audience. All appeared in the *Express & Star* with the exception of Passchendaele 1917, which is reproduced by kind permission of the *Birmingham Post & Mail*.

This book brings together some extraordinary insights into the phenomenon of armed conflict. Some of those I interviewed are famous. Some were heroes. And others, as an old soldier of D-Day once insisted I put in my notebook, were 'just participants'. Inevitably many have died since we met. They witnessed sights that my generation has been spared. They put their lives on the line for the sake of their nation, their loved ones and their mates. In the process they helped make the world a safer place.

If any one of these memories brings the enormity of warfare home to the reader in some new and unconsidered way, this book will have done its job.

Peter Rhodes
Wolverhampton
October 2009

CHAPTER ONE

A VERY VICTORIAN WAR

Memories of Khartoum

‘You can't imagine how it was, the gloom that came over people here in these streets. You would think the world had come to an end.’

John Evans recalls a national tragedy. Not the blitz of 1940, not the First World War, not even the death of Queen Victoria. One hundred and ten years old, elbow resting on the table, hand over his closed eyes, John Evans is reflecting sadly on the death of General Gordon in Khartoum. Charles George Gordon, Britain's great Imperial hero, was killed by the Mahdi's men in 1885. John Evans was eight at the time, a Welsh lad struggling with scripture texts in his native tongue at Sunday School and with the baffling constructions of the alien English language at day school. Clear as a bell in his cosy parlour warmed by an old Aga, he summons his earliest memory. It was 1882. Elsewhere, Tchaikovsky and Brahms were writing their finest works, Alexander Graham Bell was inventing the telephone and red-coated British troops were forming squares against fuzzy-wuzzy hordes in the Sudan. John Evans was five. It was his first day at school in Swansea. ‘As I went in with my teacher, Mrs Samuel, I could see big pictures on the wall of people from all round the world, black and white and brown. There was one of a Chinee with long hair and it terrified me, and I screamed until the headmistress took me away to the top of the room. I'll never forget that Chinee,’ he laughs. A deeply religious man, John Evans accepts the aches and pains of extreme old age with Biblical stoicism: ‘I don't know why God has spared me this long. I don't know whether life is given out as a share or whether you have to earn it. To be honest, you know, as I grow older I don't think too much about it at all. I treat it as a casual thing, really.' There are a number of women in the world who are older than him and several men, notably in the Georgian republic of the Soviet Union, who also claim seniority. But none can produce documentary evidence to compare with John Evans's fading hundred and ten-year-old birth certificate. He is the oldest authenticated man in the world. He worked in the mines from the age of thirteen until his retirement at seventy-three. 'It was nationalisation that did it. Suddenly they said everyone over seventy had to go. I could have gone on another ten years but we were all put out. They just gave us a bit of cardboard thanking us for our services to the coal industry.'

In a reserved occupation, John Evans was not called up to fight in the First World War, which broke out in 1914 when he was thirty-seven. 'I remember some of the boys shouting in the colliery and saying, come on, let's join up and we'll all be back home in three or four weeks. But the poor, poor dabs, they never returned . . .'He was sixty-eight when the Second World War ended with the atom-bombing of Hiroshima and Nagasaki, an event that has left him deeply fearful for the future. 'All those little children, the men and women . . . all killed, just like that. I honestly don't know if we would survive another war, with all these terrible armaments that fall from the sky.'

In all his hundred and ten years, what was the best time? 'I believe the best time was during Mr Asquith's government at the beginning of the century but before the First World War. It was an affluent time, as I remember. There was no war going on and everyone seemed contented. This was a happier country then.' *September 1987*

John Evans died on 10 June 1990, aged 112

CHAPTER TWO
THE FIRST WORLD WAR

Father goes off to war

It was another world. In her warm, cosy flat in Wolverhampton, ninety-five-year-old Clarice Onions casts her mind back to the long, hot summer of 1914. George V was on the throne. Herbert Asquith was Prime Minister. Little Clarice's father Thomas Ricketts was a twenty-seven-year-old railway worker and a former soldier, still on the reserve list. On Tuesday 4 August, the day before Clarice's sixth birthday, Britain declared war on Germany. In London the British Foreign Secretary Lord Grey remarked, 'The lights are going out all over Europe. We shall not see them lighted again in our lifetime.' Over the next four years some ten million of the brightest and best young men in Europe would be slaughtered.

Mrs Onions remembers the day as though it were yesterday: 'My mum said that Father would have to go away and, oh, I cried and cried. Father said, "I'll come back, don't worry." He was one of the first to go and he did look so smart in his uniform. I loved him so much. He was a lovely man.

'But for her younger brother, Don, the separation of war brought distress and confusion. When his father came home on leave, the little lad called him 'that man'.

The British Regular Army, dismissed by the German Kaiser as 'contemptible', was virtually wiped out in the first few weeks of the war. By Christmas it was time for Sergeant Thomas Ricketts and his comrades in the Royal Warwickshire Regiment to be sent into the trenches of the Western Front. Mrs Onions cherishes his little brass box, once containing cigarettes and chocolate, distributed to all British soldiers at Christmas 1914. By a miracle her father came through the First World War unscathed. Like many veterans of that war he rarely talked about it, but what he did describe was harrowing enough. He was a member of the so-called 'trench police', his job to ensure that, as the attack was sounded, every soldier left the trenches, even if it meant advancing to certain death in barbed wire swept by machine-guns. 'He told me that some of the soldiers would be scared and crying out for their mums. He'd say, "Come on, lads, don't think about your mothers," and make sure they went over the top.'

The First World War began when the Austrian Archduke Franz Ferdinand was assassinated while visiting the Bosnian capital, Sarajevo in June 1914. Austria demanded impossible reparations from Serbia. Germany sided with Austria. France and Russia declared support for Serbia. Russia began the slow process of mobilising her vast peasant army. Terrified of fighting on two fronts, Germany's only hope was a quick victory against France. It almost came off; but when Germany crossed the Belgian border, Britain stepped in to defend Belgium. After the first German thrust towards Paris was turned back by the 'Old Contemptibles' of the British Army, the conflict settled into the squalid business of trench warfare punctuated with occasional, enormously bloody battles.

On the home front the war brought hardships. Growing up in Stratford-upon-Avon, Clarice, her mother and brother relished rare treats such as bread smeared with lard and salt. But she recalls not a word of complaint or protest in her neighbourhood: 'It was a different world. It was just accepted that we had to beat the Germans. A lot of men came home with legs missing and a lot of girls a bit older than me never married because their fellows were killed. People were different then. They were brought up differently. I sometimes wonder how people today would have survived back then. In my day if you were told to do something you did it.' On 11 November 1918, with the British and German armies only a few miles from where they first clashed four years earlier, the Great War ended. Mrs Onions remembers Armistice Day, 1918: 'All the neighbours came out and we had a street party. They were a good lot in our street. No-one had any money or much to eat but we had a few bits and dabs of food and were quite thankful for that. After the war some people talked of going abroad for a new life but there was no money to go anywhere. They told us it was the war to end wars and there would be homes fit for heroes. But we were still as poor as church mice.' *August 2004*

A Lancer in action

In military folklore a cavalry charge is something glorious. In reality, it was a filthy, harrowing business for horse and rider alike. Jack Laiste of

Birmingham was a seventeen-year-old lancer, proudly riding off to war on his charger, Queenie. It was November 1914 in a country lane in northern France: 'All was quiet. The sun was shining. "Remount your horses" was the order. There were twenty of us. Then we saw the tip of a lance coming round the bend in the lane. It was a German cavalryman, an advance patrol. He faced us, then pulled his horse on to its haunches and turned, then all was quiet again. The squadron leader put his fingers to his mouth. Suddenly the lane widened and on a ploughed field was lined up a squadron of German cavalry with the skull and crossbones shining on their short busbies. The squadron leader shouted, "This is it!", then drew his sword and twirled it around his head. I hadn't the strength to pull my sword out of its scabbard, so I fixed my lance which was on my arm and fixed it level with Queenie's head. Not too soon. A German was making straight for me. I pulled Queenie aside as he came, and the lance went straight through him. I hadn't the strength to twist the lance and let the air into his body to withdraw the lance. The squadron leader galloping by shouted, "Pull the strap off your arm and leave the bastard with the lance in him!" Queenie was galloping along like a mad thing. I pulled on the bit but it had no effect.

'Somehow the Germans had gone. I pulled Queenie up and dismounted. She was covered with blood and white lather and I was covered with it, too. Queenie had a lump torn out of her shoulder and I had a finger hanging loose. I looked into her brown eyes. I was afraid to stroke her ears, which I used to do. I looked at her and she seemed to say, "My God, what have you done to me?" She was trembling like a leaf and so was I. I got hold of her rein and led Queenie through the dead and dying. Some tried to grab my legs and some were lying under their horses. We got to the lane where what was left of the lads had made for. My mate Jack wouldn't make it; I saw his head cut off. We went to do what we could for the Germans. We brought two back to the lane badly wounded and propped them up against the grass verge. One sank to the ground and he was calling out to me. He couldn't speak English and he pointed to his jacket where he was wounded. I pushed my hand through the sticky mess and pulled out his pay-book. There were photos inside, and he was gesticulating for me to look at them. It was his wife and children on holiday. Then he pointed to his other pocket. I pulled out an Iron Cross with the black ribbon. He wanted me to have it but I didn't want it. I felt so sick I wanted to die with him. He pointed to his chest and he pulled up a gold cross. He wanted me to hold it up, then he smiled and rolled over dead. My God, the whole world had gone mad. And just because some prince had been shot in some Balkan state.'

By a miracle, and despite three wounds, Jack Laiste survived into the 1980s when he penned this account, 'because none of the things that have been written or broadcast are anything like what the lads have been through'. *November 1998*

Sitting ducks at Gallipoli

'One Turk came at me with his bayonet, but when he was about five yards off he either stumbled or fainted so I stuck my bayonet in him. You see, we'd been told to kill or be killed, show no mercy, take no prisoners.' Terrible memories of Gallipoli come tumbling back for Sam Cutts of Penn Common, the last Black Country survivor of the Dardanelles campaign: 'We went ashore and there was one or two shots coming our way but nothing hit us. We'd only gone about thirty yards when we saw a Turkish patrol,' says Mr Cutts, one hundred years old. 'And straightaway our officers told us to dig in.' For the untried soldiers of the South Staffordshire Regiment's seventh battalion, it was the first mistake in a campaign littered with errors of judgement. For as they dug in at Suvla bay, the Turkish patrol escaped. By the time the battalion advanced the Turks were waiting in force.'

It was terrible, terrible. The trenches were full of bodies. The Turks had poisoned a well with two bodies. They were a cruel lot, the Turks. They maimed some of our prisoners and sent them back. It was awful, the smell and the bluebottles on the bodies. The trench had a rocky bottom so we couldn't bury them. We just had to cover the bodies with sandbags. The Turks were on the hills and we were below, sitting ducks; the snipers were shooting us like rabbits. Twenty lads I knew personally were killed and we lost all our officers.' In the blazing Turkish summer the men of the South Staffs fell ill from infected water. As winter fell they were so cold that some actually welcomed lice: 'Scratching them at night was the only way to keep warm.' Sam Cutts from Penn Common, survived Gallipoli, only to be wounded by shrapnel at Arras and by a bullet through the arm on the Somme. But his bitterest memories are of Gallipoli and, whatever the historians say, he pins the blame on its architect. 'I blame Churchill. It was his fault . . . he made a blunder.' *April 1990*

The carnage of Loos

These are their blue remembered hills. The slopes rise high above Sedbergh, peaks lost in the boiling mists of an autumn squall. In the valley is Sedbergh School, a grim old grey-stone pile. Along the dripping road leading to it, thin figures in singlets and shorts are cross-country racing, hair rain-plastered on their foreheads. This is a place where, since 1525, boys have been turned into men on a diet of fresh air, exercise and muscular Christianity, and sent to do their nation's bidding. The school's Latin motto says it all: '*Dura Virum Nutrix*' – 'A stern nurse of men'. One hundred years ago three Black Country brothers were sent to stern Sedbergh and became stars of the school. Their father was John Perks Shaw, a wealthy hardware merchant in Wolverhampton. The 1901 Census shows that by the age of fifty-one Shaw had made his money and retired, and was living in some style with his wife Eliza at West Bank, a huge house in Richmond Road. They had three sons: Hamilton, born in 1879; Malcolm, born in 1888; and Leslie, born two years later. Hamilton was first to enter Sedbergh, excelling in school sports in the 1890s. After school he went on to play rugby for England in the 1906/07 season.

By that time the two younger brothers were at Sedbergh for a couple of years of finishing after a spell at Wolverhampton Grammar School. The Black Country lads loved it. From the school records: 'The fells for ten miles round know well the strenuous performances of this hardy trio.'

Elspeth Griffiths, the school archivist, lovingly turns the pages. They tell how Leslie entered in September 1905. By Christmas he was third in the class; by the next summer he was top. Military training was an obligation. A scrapbook photo shows tall young Leslie as part of an award-winning drill squad. It was the age of Empire. These public-school boys were disciplined and fiercely patriotic, but they were not robots. They rebelliously carved their names in any exposed woodwork, and accepted the inevitable caning with good grace. One of Leslie Shaw's contemporaries, Leslie Duckworth, fed up with the local church bells, famously took a rifle and shot both hands off the clock.'

He'll have to be expelled,' declared the headmaster.'But it's Bisley next week,' protested the housemaster, horrified at losing such a crack shot before the famous rifle competition. 'Very well,' conceded the head. 'A good beating will suffice.'

When war came, a few years later, nothing could keep men like this from the fray. They volunteered in their thousands, and perished in droves. The slaughter of England's elite was cruel. Of the sixty-two boys who left Sedbergh in the year 1911 alone, twenty were killed in the war.

The school's memorial cloisters bear the names of 453 who perished in the First and Second World Wars. L.G. Shaw is among them. He was one of those fine young Edwardian gentlemen whose only fear in the summer of 1914 was that the Great War would be over before they got to the front. Training as an officer would have wasted precious time, so he signed up as a humble squaddie, Private 9390 Shaw of the South Staffordshire Regiment. He would have stood out. In 1914 the public-school classes were on average five inches taller than working-class lads from the inner cities. 'Too tall for my trench,' one Old Sedberghian

7

wrote to his school. On 30 August 1915 Leslie Gardner Shaw was commissioned as an officer in the South Staffords' 5th Battalion. Six weeks later he was dead. The twenty-five-year-old officer fell with hundreds of North and South Staffords men in the infamous 13 October attack on the Hohenzollern Redoubt, a German strongpoint, during the battle of Loos. It was the Black Country's bloodiest day of the war. The British artillery hardly damaged the German trenches. As soon as the barrage stopped, German machine-guns swept the British parapets. The men knew they had to climb out of the trenches into this murderous hail. According to reports, not one flinched. Sedbergh's book of military honours records that a former pupil met Lieutenant Shaw shortly before his death and noted 'his utter disregard for either personal safety or comfort, so long as our cause was progressing satisfactorily. On October 13, in the afternoon, when leading his platoon against the Hohenzollern Redoubt he was shot through the head by machine-gun fire.'

Leslie Shaw's body, like thousands of others, was never found. His two brothers also served in the war. Malcolm was wounded in 1917 but survived. Hamilton came home unscathed. Their grief-stricken parents paid for a stained-glass window in memory of their youngest son at Wombourne United Reformed Church. On Remembrance Sunday 2005 the restored cloisters at Sedbergh School were rededicated to the memory of the old boys who never came home. Among the far-off fells he loved, a Black Country hero was remembered again. *October 2005*

Bombed by a Zeppelin

There's one thing about being bombed by a Zeppelin: you never forget it. Len Turner of Lower Penn remembers every detail: 'I was just six. We heard this noise in the sky and we all looked up. There was this huge object. It seemed only a few hundred feet up. I could clearly see two men in a basket container underneath. They were dropping things out over the side. Of course, we hadn't a clue what they were.'

Young Len was an eyewitness to the terrifying dawn of the air-raid age. It was the night of 31 January 1916. High above, Zeppelin L.21 was commanded by Kapitanleutnant Max Dietrich, whose orders were to bomb Liverpool. He was hopelessly lost. As young Len and his neighbours watched, Dietrich's crew began dropping bombs. By the end of that night Tipton, Bradley, Wednesbury and Walsall had been hit. Thirty-five local people were killed. As the explosions began the mood in Tipton changed from curiosity to terror.

'We ran for a cellar. I remember two things just like it was yesterday. There was this old lady in the street, terrified, hysterical, pulling her dress up to cover her face. Of course, her underwear was exposed and she was crying, "Oh don't look, men, don't look, I can't help it." Inside the cellar there were candles lit and I saw this real thug from our street, a man who was always beating his wife. Well, he was on his knees praying out loud.'

Like many families the terrified Turners had no father to protect them. Charles, an insurance agent, had volunteered at the start of the war and was away in France. 'I remember when he went, my mother cried a bit. But she always tried to hide her face from us. She was a very brave and wonderful woman.'

Charles joined the South Staffordshire Regiment. His war ended with a grisly back wound on the Somme in northern France. He spent months in hospital and the wound refused to heal. It needed dressing twice a day, almost until the old man died in the 1970s. 'Yet he never breathed a word of complaint. He was a marvellous man.'

The soldiers were promised homes fit for heroes but Britain emerged into post-war poverty. Charles Turner had a tiny army pension and took work first as a church caretaker. 'At the age of ten I was working with him. It was hard work, too, carrying the water in buckets to fill the tank and fetching coke into the cellar for the boiler.' In the Second World War Len Turner was an instructor on Churchill tanks. He has lived a remarkable life from the horse-drawn age to the internet, from poverty to wealth. But his clearest memory of all is that vast, cigar-shaped balloon in the skies above Tipton all those years ago.
August 2004

The Somme

Basil Houle was a child of Imperial Britain, the son of a London solicitor and a chorister at St George's Chapel, Windsor. In 1910 he sang at the funeral of Edward VII and at the Coronation of George V and Queen Mary. Four years later the First World War broke out and young Basil, with millions of others, joined the mad rush to the colours. 'I was seventeen but I told them I was eighteen,' he recalls at his home in Tettenhall, Wolverhampton. 'I couldn't get in quickly enough. Our only worry was that the war might be over by the time we got there!'

By the end of 1915 Rifleman 2012 Houle of the 1st London Rifle Brigade was in trenches in Belgium. It was hardly the war he had imagined. 'We did two weeks on, two weeks off in the trenches. You just sat there on the fire step with your feet in water and went to sleep. I never even fired a shot.'

But things soon changed. He became a sniper and his unit, part of 56th (London) Division, moved to the gentle downland near the river Somme in northern France. They began training for the biggest British offensive of the war. The aim was to destroy the formidable German defences with artillery fire. Then the British forces, including the untried youngsters of Kitchener's New Army, would simply walk forward and seize the trenches. If all went well the war could be over in weeks. Basil recalls the optimism as his battalion, loaded with weapons, signposts, barbed wire and ladders, endlessly rehearsed its moves over practice trenches miles behind the lines. The battle of the Somme was heralded by a week-long artillery bombardment. The young soldiers watched in amazement as millions of shells crashed down on the German lines a few hundred yards away. 'I wasn't a bit frightened. Why should we be? We hadn't seen anything to be apprehensive about. Why, on the night before the attack I just sat on the back of the trench and watched the shelling.'

At 7.30am on Saturday 1 July the whistles blew and along the 18-mile front a hundred thousand soldiers climbed out of their trenches and advanced. The 56th was at the far north of the battle in a diversionary attack on a German position at Gommecourt Wood. It was reckoned to be the best Territorial division in the battle and fought well, capturing all the German front-line trenches. 'We dug ourselves in, the sunshine came out and it was a beautiful morning. We more or less lay there sunbathing. There was a lot of firing further down the line but not much near us.' In their tiny sector Rifleman Houle and his pals had no idea of the catastrophe around them. Despite the bombardment, despite the promises of the generals, the defenders were not wiped out. As the British advanced they were mown down in waves by German machine-guns and shells. The British attacks to the right of the London Division faded away. The inevitable German counter-attack followed. 'Suddenly we could see the Germans moving up the trenches towards us. I shot one and he went down shouting. Another one looked round and I got him in the back. I got so mad and excited, I could have killed the Kaiser and everybody else. But they came back and absolutely showered us with bombs, so we all scrambled back towards our own lines.'

As he moved back Basil Houle was hit by shrapnel from a British shell. Paralysed and exhausted, he dragged himself into a shell hole. To escape the bullets he had to lie on a dead body, 'the most horrible experience of my life'. As darkness fell he was spotted by a German soldier and carried into captivity. After a spell in hospital he was put to work in a German coal mine for the rest of the war.

'It all started with such high hopes, but everything was so badly organised. Looking back, I realise that if I hadn't been captured I would not be here today.' He is almost certainly right. Basil Houle's 1st London Rifle Brigade numbered 800 men at dawn on 1 July 1916. By the end of the day 572 were dead, wounded or missing. Other battalions suffered even worse fates, the Accrington Pals losing 585, the Newfoundland Regiment 684 and the 10th West Yorkshires 710. British casualties totalled 60,000. It was the worst single day in our military history. In the space of eight hours the British Army suffered more casualties than in the Crimean, Boer and Korean wars combined. No battle in history had such a shattering effect on Britain. The cream of towns and cities was wiped out in the first day of the Somme. Yorkshire suffered 9,000 killed, Lancashire 6,000, London 5,500, Birmingham more than 1,000, and so on and on. Hardly a family was untouched by the disaster.

'After the war was over I took part in a march through London with my regiment. There was not a single, solitary soul that I knew. God knows what happened to the rest.' *June 1986*

Private Alvin Smith's war

Lothersdale, North Yorkshire: This is where it began, in a village where the Smiths had farmed for generations. At Christmas 1915 Alvin Smith, the nineteen-year-old son of farmer Edmund and Sarah Jane Smith was walking with his girlfriend, Amy. The First World War had been raging for more than a year. Alvin's brother, John (my grandfather), had joined up at the start, but Alvin had been needed to help run Burlington Farm. His dad insisted. It was an embarrassing position, as all the best chaps seemed to be in khaki. It would not take much to make Alvin defy his parents. At Christmas it came.

'Would you love me if I was a soldier?' Alvin joked as he walked with Amy.

'Well,' teased the pretty eighteen-year-old, in a reply that was to haunt her for the next eighty years, 'I might respect you a bit more.'

Respect. That did it. Over Christmas dinner with friends and family, Alvin turned to his best pal, Willie Smith, and said, 'We'd better enjoy this Christmas, Willie, because we probably won't see the next one.'

'There was nothing dramatic about the way he said it,' Amy told me many years later. 'It was just a statement of fact.'

Alvin and Willie enlisted together on 29 January 1916, as privates in the Duke of Wellington's Regiment (West Riding). They were innocents in arms, rushed over to France after a frantic few weeks of training to take part in the long-awaited British offensive, which was already being called The Big Push. Soon it would be known by a name that became a byword for slaughter: the Somme.

Thiepval, the Somme: This is where it ended, a placid corner of northern France where the autumn sun blazes down on dry, new-ploughed fields and the potato harvest is piled in tons beside the farm tracks. The scars of the 1916 trenches can still be seen and every year's ploughing uncovers the 'iron harvest' of unexploded shells. A few years ago, walking the route that Private Alvin Smith and his pals followed, I found something white sticking out of the earth bank of a sunken track. As I pulled it, eighteen inches of human thigh bone emerged, a reminder of the carnage on these gentle chalk slopes. In 1916 the Germans held the high ground here, commanding every hill-top and valley slope. The village of Thiepval and the 1,000-yard-long Thiepval Spur, which stuck like a giant finger into the British lines, were bristling with concrete gun emplacements, trenches and deep dugouts, all screened behind vast hedges of barbed wire. Alvin's battalion, the 1st/7th, was in reserve on the terrible first day of the Somme on 1 July 1916, and was spared the horror that left 20,000 young Britons dead and 40,000 wounded. Alvin's friend, Willie Smith, was reported killed on 7 July.

The division got its first blooding in an attack on 3 September. It failed wretchedly. The British commander-in-chief, General Sir Douglas Haig, was furious. He wrote scathingly in his diary, 'The total losses of this division are less than 1,000!' In the grim arithmetic of the Somme, where every yard was measured in deaths, the West Riding lads were not dying quickly enough. To infuriate the top brass further, some of the division's troops had failed to salute a visiting general, which probably explains the terse entry in the 1st/7th Battalion's diary for 8 September: 'Games before breakfast followed by saluting drill.'

On 15 September another Yorkshire battalion seized German trenches south of Thiepval. Three companies of Alvin's battalion, about 700 men, moved forward that night to take over the trenches and prepare for another attack. It began, disastrously, at 6pm on Sunday 17 September with a terrible misjudgement. The battalion's mortars got the range wrong and hit their own trenches, exploding a store of hand grenades. Amid the dead and wounded and the confusion of this 'friendly fire' incident, a Captain Lupton calmly climbed on to the trench parapet and heroically rallied the men.

The attack was all over in an hour. It was such a success that a general visited the battalion two days later to offer his congratulations. The West Riding lads had advanced 350 feet beyond their objective. In doing so they lost 220 men. The arithmetic of the Somme was working. They never found Alvin's body. During a lull in the fighting one of his mates went back for water. When he returned the captured trench had been found by German guns and the occupants blown to shreds. The name of Private Alvin Smith is recorded on the Thiepval memorial to those who died on the Somme and who have no known grave. There are 73,000 names. A few days after his death, the local newspaper in Yorkshire recorded: 'He was well known in the village and district and was highly esteemed by all who knew him. He was a well-built youth, of a pleasant and cheerful disposition.' *September 1996*

Burial duty

In tiny, painstaking print the grisly life of a First World War soldier springs from the curling pages of a little diary. Percy 'Ginger' Guest of West Bromwich volunteered and, in December 1915, joined the Royal Warwickshire Regiment. Soon he was in France as part of a pioneer party that recovered the dead for burial.

'He told us about going out into no-man's land and picking up dead bodies, and parts of bodies,' says his grand-daughter Maureen South. 'It was a horrible job and no-one wanted to do it.'

Corporal Guest's diary is cherished by his daughter, Edna Whitehouse of Wall Heath, Dudley. As she turns the pages the horror of trench warfare is revealed. On 1 July 1916 the British launched the battle of the Somme. In the first few hours 20,000 Tommies were killed. Corporal Guest wrote: '19 July: Rushed up in buses to Laventie to reinforce 6 and 7 Battalions. Stopped at Masselot Redoubt, burying dead for several days. 25 July: Went back to line with Chaplain to identify graves. Got back 10.30pm. 4 August: Went again with Chaplain to fix crosses.'

His war ended on 11 December 1917, near the French town of Fricourt. His diary contains one word: 'Gassed.'

'Ginger' spent months recovering from mustard gas and, despite permanent lung damage, lived until he was eighty-seven, passing away in 1982. Like many Great War soldiers, he told his wife and children little of the horrors he had seen. But after the Second World War had ended in Europe a family tragedy opened the floodgates. Mr Guest's younger son, James, was an officer with the RAF, stationed in India. On 18 June 1945 he was killed in a flying accident. Edna recalls: 'My father never talked about the war when we were young. But in his later years, after his son was killed, he started thinking about all those things again.'

For the first time the family became aware of the grisly job their father had done in France. It explained the caption on a photograph of him with four colleagues: 'The Angelic Five'. Edna says: 'Sometimes in his diary he just wrote "bad day". That was when a lot of chaps had been killed and he just wanted to wipe it out of his mind.'

The early work of recovering and identifying bodies on the battlefields of the Western Front in 1914–18, recovering identity tags and planting crosses, made possible the immaculate war cemeteries visited by millions of relatives and tourists today. *August 2004*

Passchendaele

For Fred Cowles the Great War ended in a muddy crater in the no-man's land beyond Ypres. It was 22 August 1917 and his unit, the 6th Battalion the Border Regiment, had gone over the top in yet another of those bloody, futile rushes at the German lines that typified the horrific battle of Passchendaele.

Private 21853 Cowles took cover in a crater two feet deep in liquid mud to give covering fire for advancing soldiers. 'My corporal, Dick Nuttall, was using the Lewis gun. He fired about twenty magazines then said, "Here, Fred, you have a go at this." I stepped forward and he stepped backward to exactly where I had been. Three minutes later we were both on the ground. He was dead and I was hit in the leg and elbow.'

As he was stretchered to the rear by four shocked soldiers, Fred Cowles saw the shattered hulk of Ypres Cloth Hall above him. His elbow healed but his left leg was beyond help. On 2 January 1918 it was amputated. 'But when I dream, I'm walking, running or jumping, just like before.'

John Powell was a signaller with a Royal Field Artillery battery and was repairing buried telephone lines near Passchendaele when his number came up. 'Five of us were out and Jerry sent over a 5.9 inch shell. There was some Notts & Derby lads going up the trenches and we all heard this shell coming. Then it burst over us. It knocked us all out. Six were killed but God must have been with two or three of us because we lived.' Barely conscious, he was shipped back to the base at Etaples, to the most horrifying of experiences. For the medics had taken him for dead. 'When I woke up I was in the morgue. There were all these chaps covered in blankets on stretchers resting on trestles in this whacking great tent. I pushed the blanket off my face and two stretcher bearers saw me. They nearly died of shock.'

It was a further five days before the young soldier awoke fully from his coma. After convalescing in England he was shipped to France to help stem the German offensive of spring 1918. He recalls the end of the war on 11 November 1918 as though it happened yesterday. 'We were near the German border by then. It was bitterly cold. The signaller came out and said, "Eleven o'clock – it's all over at eleven". There was not one cry of joy. We wanted to finish the job, all the way to Berlin.'

John Powell recalls trench life vividly: 'It was just mud and slush. We were alive with lice and I had forty-eight boils at one time. We became callous towards death. You took no notice of it, except when it came to the animals. I remember a sergeant-major saying to me, "We can get you buggers for a shilling a day but the horses cost eighty quid each."' *August 1983*

Huj: the last cavalry charge

It was 8 November 1917 and things were at last going well for the British in their long, bloody war in Palestine. The Turks, allies of Germany, had been beaten at Gaza and were withdrawing toward

Jerusalem. But as the 60th (London) Division advanced on the small town of Huj, they found the way blocked by a mixed force of Turkish and German gunners. Unable to move, the Londoners called for the cavalry. And the scene was set for the last classic cavalry charge in the history of the British Army.

On a dusty ridge in the Holy Land, outnumbered ten to one, the riders faced the blazing muzzles of cannon. It was a scene that had hardly changed since the Charge of the Light Brigade sixty-three years earlier. Even the distance of half a league (1½ miles) was the same. The difference was that this charge was carried out not by the cream of the regular cavalry but by a couple of yeomanry units from the West Midlands. They were ploughboys and factory hands who had learned their sword and saddle skills on drill nights and weekends around Warwick, Stratford, Dudley and Stourbridge as part of the Territorial Army.

At the word of command this force of twelve officers and 158 men drew their swords and galloped against the guns and a mass of two thousand Turkish soldiers. Darcy Harold Jones, the last survivor of the charge, who died in 1997, recalled an officer shouting, 'It's the guns we're after, lads!' The *Express & Star*'s report a few days later told how the Midland horsemen attacked 'with a full-throated cheer'. The Turks, with German and Austrian advisers, stood their ground, firing shells at point-blank range. One group of the Worcestershire Yeomanry rode straight at the main Turkish infantry force. The rest, joined by the Warwickshire Yeomanry and spurred on by their officers' hunting horns, thundered into the artillery lines, scattering the gunners. Author Colin Smith researched the charge for the climax in his novel, *The Last Crusade*. He interviewed some of the last survivors to create this dramatic image. Weidinger, a German staff officer, witnesses the charge: 'They were not coming in the way Weidinger had always imagined a cavalry charge, a great glorious mass of men and horseflesh advancing on the enemy stirrup to stirrup. They looked more like Cossacks than regular cavalry, and every few seconds they would vanish into their own dust.'

A Yeomanry officer in the frontline of the charge, W.B. Mercer, wrote: 'Machine guns and rifles opened on us the moment we topped the rise. I remember thinking that the sound of the crackling bullets was just like a hailstorm on an iron-topped building. A whole heap of men and horses went down thirty yards from the muzzles of the gun. The squadron seemed to melt away completely. For a time at any rate I had the impression that I was the only man alive.'

It was all over in twenty minutes. Twenty-six Yeomen died in the charge and forty were wounded. One hundred horses perished, some killed by shells that passed straight through them before exploding. Yet the attack succeeded. And even in the blood-lust, mercy was shown. Seventy prisoners were taken, together with eleven guns, one of which has pride of place in the Warwickshire Yeomanry Museum, Warwick.

The Warwickshire and Worcestershire Yeomanry were attached to an Australian force, whose official history recorded: 'This charge had taken place in full view of the Australians who were quick to appreciate the fact that the British Territorial horsemen could no longer be estimated lightly as campaigners.'

The charge at Huj was not the last cavalry action of the war. Some Australian cavalry later charged, brandishing bayonets. Some British riders harassed the Germans in France right up to the Armistice on 11 November 1918. But Huj was the last occasion when British cavalrymen, without any supporting fire, charged enemy guns and took them at sword point. The traditions of the regiments that charged at Huj are continued today by two TA units, the Royal Mercian & Lancastrian Yeomanry and 67 (Queen's Own Warwickshire & Worcestershire Yeomanry) Signal Squadron. All these years after the charge at Huj, the memory is potent. Major Malcolm Cooper of Stourbridge, a former officer with 67 Signal Squadron who commanded a signal squadron in Bosnia, says the spirit of Huj is alive and well among today's TA Yeomen: 'The traditions of the unit and its history are important when the chips are down and you need to cling to something to help pull you through. It is all too easy to cast aside tradition. History of the unit should be passed on. We remember the charge at Huj with great pride.' *November 2007*

The Kaiser's fleet is scuttled

The last victims of the First World War were a group of unarmed German sailors who dared to sink their own ships. It was Midsummer's Day in June 1919. The Kaiser's once-proud High Seas Fleet had been impounded in the Royal Navy port of Scapa Flow in the Orkneys for months since the Armistice. Suddenly ships' bells rang out across the seventy moored warships. Crews began to abandon the vessels. Within minutes, to the astonishment of children on a sightseeing boat, the entire fleet began to sink 'like some macabre steel water-ballet', as author Tony Booth puts it.

On the orders of their commander, the Germans had sunk their own ships. When they refused Royal Navy orders to get back on board and save them, the shooting began. Nine Germans were killed and sixteen wounded as British sailors opened fire. At his home in Guernsey, Tony Booth has no doubt that these were war crimes 'for which the Royal Navy has never answered. To make it worse the whole thing was witnessed by children.'

Britain was horrified, not by the shootings but by the scuttling. 'Huns to the last' snarled the *Express & Star* headline. Booth takes up the story five years later, when the sunken fleet, thought to be worthless, was bought by Ernest Cox, a scrap dealer in far-off Wolverhampton. For years the price he paid the Admiralty was a secret. Booth, searching through old records, believes it was £24,000, less than £1 million at today's values. Salvage experts at the time said it was impossible to raise so many big ships from a deep anchorage. But Ernest Cox, born in 1883 in a small Victorian house in Wolverhampton, did not understand the word 'impossible'.

He developed a process of pumping air into the ships' hulls to re-float them. As the locals gasped in amazement, ship after ship came bobbing to the surface to be beached and cut up for scrap. Cox's greatest feat was to raise the 28,000-ton battleship *Hindenburg* from 70 feet of water. The raising of the German Fleet at Scapa Flow stands as the greatest maritime salvage operation of all time. Tony Booth traced some of the metal to knives and forks in the United States, and much was used in post-war Britain. But a substantial amount was sold, via a third party, to Krupps and other German armaments firms in the 1930s. Some of Ernest Cox's steel salvaged from the wreckage of the First World War was recycled and, with supreme irony, used against the British in the Second World War. *June 2008*

CHAPTER THREE
THE SECOND WORLD WAR

The Holocaust begins

Sit down on the floor. Arms folded across your chest, backs of knees hard against the floor. How long before the pain defeats you? After a few minutes the man in front of Leon Jessel gave up. As he moved his arms in agony a Nazi soldier smashed his head with the steel-shod butt of a Mauser rifle. 'His skull just split open. His brains flew over me. They were still twitching.'

In his first three days at Buchenwald concentration camp, the twenty-year-old Jew saw 300 of his group killed. 'Some were shot. Most were beaten to death, usually kicked between the abdomen and knees. I had a lot of courage before I went to Buchenwald. Afterwards, none.' His is a story to make your heart weep, and yet only once does he come close to crying. A tear, more of rage and disgust than of sorrow, sparkles in his left eye. 'Do you know, I have seen men beating other men to death and getting sexual excitement out of it. I mean, all the way. Foaming at the mouth . . .' He has seen mankind at its worst and best. He will never forget the taxi driver who risked arrest by spiriting him out of town as the Nazis rounded up the first batches of Jews. Or the woman on a train who saw – and smelt – him in his filthy, diarrhoea-soaked clothes and knew he was a victim of the Nazis, but insisted on sharing her bread and milk with him. But he can never forget, or forgive, the good citizens of Frankfurt who, as his group of Jews were led away to captivity, pelted them with bricks and boiling water. 'Why? Why would they do that?'

Leon Jessel grew up in Duisburg, the son of a Jewish shopkeeper. As the Nazis swept to power, Jew-hating became Germany's national obsession. 'At school, our teacher told the class that Jews were bad, criminals, bastards, and you could tell them by their black hair, bent backs and crooked noses. I pointed out that I was blond, my nose was perfectly normal and I was a first-class sportsman. He threw me out of the class.'

For twenty-eight days in the summer of 1938 he escaped the nightmare. An apprentice leather-worker, he came to England for one month's work experience. Once back in Germany he dodged the inevitable for a few days, living rough and sleeping in parks. The Gestapo caught up with him at a relative's house. The knock at the door: 'Are you Jewish?'

'Yes.'

'Are you really Jewish?' The Gestapo were taken aback by his blond hair.

'Yes.'

'You had better come with us.'

He was taken to Buchenwald concentration camp with its regime of starvation, dehydration and random killing. 'After three days you were no longer a human being. They built a gallows and hanged two lads who had killed a guard. To my eternal shame I chewed a piece of bread as I watched. By then I had eaten the leather flap of my briefcase.'

He survived three months in Buchenwald before being freed in one of the token releases of prisoners organised for Nazi propaganda. Filthy, lousy, shaven-headed, he returned home briefly. Somehow, a visa was arranged and in February 1939 – seven months before the Second World War began – Leon Jessel took the train to Holland, thence to England. He recalls his final parting from his father: 'I told him everything I had seen. He cried with me, because a boy of twenty should not see such things.'

After the war Mr Jessel discovered that his father and mother had been killed in the gas chambers of Auschwitz. His sister Ruth was burned alive, aged twenty-seven, when the Nazis torched another death camp. Hitler's Holocaust killed about six million Jews, including sixteen of the Jessel family.

'Why not me?' muses the old man in Walsall. 'There's no reason. There but for the grace of God . . .' Leon Jessel married, became a respected leather manufacturer, a magistrate and Freemason. But he never spoke publicly about his ordeal until 1997 when, as part of Walsall's Anne Frank exhibition, he addressed a capacity audience at the town's Leather Museum. Why wait so long? 'Because the line between truth and lie is so fine,' he answers simply. For all the evil done to him, he never wanted to demonise the entire German race. That would be a generalisation, the sort of thinking that led directly to the Holocaust.

And could a Holocaust come again? 'Oh yes. The inhumanity of human beings to human beings knows no frontiers. There is nothing worse than the human species. And yet there must be some good, otherwise humanity would have stopped existing a long, long time ago. There must be more good than evil, mustn't there?' *June 1997*

The day war broke out

'I remember it as if it were yesterday,' says Mary Seabrook. 'The news came over the radio and my mother, who had lived through the First World War, just burst into tears. And because she wept so did I. It was terrible. We didn't know what to expect.' Meanwhile, a hundred miles away in London, young Bert Seabrook was off for a Sunday morning drink. Suddenly the first air-raid sirens sounded. After some thought Bert carried on. No point in letting a war get in the way of a pint. Neither could have guessed that the cataclysm of the next six years – and a German gunner – would bring them together.

In 1940 Bert Seabrook was called up into the Royal Berkshires. He served as a Desert Rat in the North Africa campaign and survived the battle of El Alamein plus two invasions, first in Sicily and later in the D-Day landings of June 1944. His luck ran out two months later in Normandy when he was hit in the head and hands by shrapnel from a German shell. Evacuated to England, he was recovering in Stafford hospital when a party of ATS girls, including Mary, came visiting. The couple hit it off immediately. Mary had been called up two years earlier, serving as a teleprinter operator with the Royal Signals in London and York. They married after six months, 'because they were sending ATS girls abroad and we wanted to stay together. In those days you had to live every minute and snatch every bit of happiness,' she says at her home in Brewood. 'People made friends all the time, on train journeys and so on. Everybody seemed to have this sense of comradeship and pulling together. What's happened to it now? I really don't know.' *April 1989*

The Territorials go to war

They still call it 'the longest summer camp ever'. For many lads in the 1930s the Territorial Army offered a little pocket money and the promise of a fortnight's annual camp away from the grime of town and city. But in the first few days of September 1939 the government suddenly called in the chips. The citizen soldiers, some only sixteen, were embodied for regular service. For some, like the Terriers of the South Staffordshire Regiment on camp at Gower, it was straight into a spell of intensive training for the battle of France. Others saw the call-up announced in the newspaper or heard it on the radio, and reported to their drill halls more out of curiosity than war-lust.

Young Ken Owen of Bradmore, Wolverhampton, dawdled on his way to the Staffordshire Yeomanry riding school at Newhampton Road.

'It was my girlfriend's birthday and pay day, too. So I went into town to buy her a present, and then to the Queen's Cinema, with the result that I was the last to report. Bill Cope, our sergeant-major, greeted me with, "Oh, so you've finally decided to come!"'

The squadron moved off to Welbeck Abbey where Ken met up with his brothers, Ben and Eddie, also serving in the Yeomanry. But while older brother Ben went off to war with rifle and sabre in Palestine, Ken and Eddie could only watch the great adventure with envy. Both were held back in Britain because they were too young for active service. Ken saw his share of action later, as a sergeant in the East Surreys, fighting in the Middle East, Italy and Greece. Thankfully, all three brothers came through the war unscathed.

On 3 September 1939 a young officer, Peter Windridge, assistant adjutant with the South Staffs 6th Battalion, stood in Princes Square, Wolverhampton, as Neville Chamberlain's fateful broadcast was relayed over the loudspeakers. 'It was a lovely, mellow morning. When the news came, the overall feeling was of relief, a sort of restrained delight that at last we were telling Hitler where to get off.'

Eight months later, in the retreat to Dunkirk, the twenty-five-year-old captain earned the dubious distinction of being the first Wolverhampton soldier to be seriously wounded. Almost killed in a dive-bomb attack, he was put aboard the last hospital ship to leave Dunkirk, and survived to end the war in the army's West Africa headquarters.

For bus driver Claude Parrott of West Bromwich, the Second World War began when a dispatch rider pulled up alongside his bus in Great Bridge and told him to report to his drill hall in Carters Green, at the double. Claude, a sergeant in a Territorial unit of the Royal Army Service Corps, had to leave his bus-load of passengers and dash off to war. He saw action in North Africa and Italy. For the Parrotts, like so many others, the war was a family affair. Father Charles was too old for the army but served in the Home Guard. Claude's brother, Frank, was a lieutenant in the Green Howards and was killed at Rangoon in 1944. Sisters Dorothy and Gladys served with the WAAF while the youngest sisters, Christine and Helen, were evacuated to Lichfield.

For Harry Rawlings, a nineteen-year-old in the Seventh Battalion the Worcestershire Regiment, news of war came after church parade at Oldbury parish church. 'We had been mobilised on the Friday, 1 September, and on the Sunday we marched back from the church to Langley drill hall. All the mothers and families were outside in tears, saying that war had been declared. We didn't feel too bright but we soon got over it.' Driven back to Dunkirk in the fall of France, Mr Rawlings of Maypole Road, Oldbury, remembers the men who crewed the little boats in the rescue fleet. 'I still think the world of them. And the men on the beach.'

For Private 4915251 Albert Smith of Bilston, war came at the end of annual camp with C (Bilston) Company of the 6th Battalion the South Staffordshire Regiment in Gower. The eighteen-year-old and his pals went straight into infantry training and had their baptism of fire with the British Expeditionary Force in France in early 1940. Forced back by the Panzers, the South Staffs found themselves on the beach at Dunkirk. 'It was chaos. We dug a trench in the sand and suddenly the bombers came over and buried us. We had to dig ourselves out with our hands. After Dunkirk I don't think we really thought about winning or losing. We were all so young. We just took everything as it came.'

Bert Foster, of Whitmore Reans, joined the TA in 1938 as a private in the South Staffs. 'My father had served in the Great War and we both followed the news. My father said "We're here again" and we both knew there was a war coming.'

Mr Foster recalls the terror of being shelled and bombed – he still suffers from nerves – and the extraordinary spirit after being evacuated from Dunkirk. 'There was bunting everywhere and people were saying, 'Well done, boys, it's good to have you back.' It was as though we'd won the war.'Private Foster served in the North Africa campaign and was captured in 1942. But he escaped from a POW camp in Italy and, assisted by friendly Partisans, trekked over the Alps to safety in Switzerland.

For Charles Evans of Penn the enduring image of the war is the Nazi death camp at Belsen. As a corporal medic he was part of the British team responsible for documenting the survivors and burying an estimated thirty thousand dead in mass graves. 'I was only twenty-three at the time and I suppose I was hardened to it. But you can't forget it. It's still so vivid. I still get the smell of it, even now.'

Mr Evans joined up at Mander Street, Wolverhampton, four months before the outbreak of war and spent the early years providing medical cover for anti-aircraft batteries in Britain. As part of a field hospital in the rear of the Normandy invasion and the Rhine crossings, he witnessed appalling injuries. Yet his most vivid memory is of man's inhumanity to man behind the barbed wire of Belsen.

As Neville Chamberlain announced the outbreak of war on the radio, Daisy Howard of Bilston wept. After the Munich crisis a year before, Chamberlain had promised 'peace in our time'. Only then had Mrs Howard allowed her two lads, Jack, eighteen, and seventeen-year-old Bill, to join the Territorials. Now, on the day war broke out, they were due back from annual TA camp at Gower with the South Staffordshire Regiment. But as the afternoon wore on there was no sign of them.

Mrs Howard was distraught. With good reason. 'I remember the First World War. I'd seen the Territorials marching off to war in August 1914, all good young men. So many of them didn't come back. We waited and waited for Jack and Bill to come home and then I said, "That's it – they're off to France." I thought we'd never see them again.' Finally, after a desperate search, she found the battalion billeted at Penkridge. 'They were only boys. I remember our youngest was ready to cry, with big beads of sweat on his face.'

Jack was soon in action in France with the British Expeditionary Force. Evacuated from Dunkirk in 1940, he was later in the thick of the Italian campaign. Because of his age, Bill was kept in Britain until the D-Day invasion of France in 1944. Ironically, while neither brother suffered a scratch, Mrs Howard was wounded by a piece of shrapnel during an air raid in 1942. 'I remember her face covered in blood,' says her daughter, Dorothy. 'I just cried and cried.' *September 1989*

A slave for Stalin

A knock on the farmhouse door. Outside were two Russian soldiers, rifles at the ready. They told the family to gather their belongings and prepare to move. But the family, like so many in Poland in 1940, was already scattered. Father had already been interrogated by the Soviets and had fled for the relative safety of the German sector. Older sister Janina was staying the night with a friend.

Twelve-year-old Henryka, her older brother Stanislaw and their mother were loaded on to a sledge with their pitiful bundles of clothes. Tears come to the eyes of Mrs Henryka Lappo in the dining room of her home in Wolverhampton as she recalls that bitter night in February 1940 after Hitler and Stalin had carved up Poland. 'I remember the Russian troops marching in. I can still smell them, the smell of the tar they used to blacken their boots. On 10 February came the banging on the door. Everywhere in our village it was the same. Mother was so brave. She thought they would take us into the wood and shoot us. At least our sister would be all right. We were so shocked, terrified and cold that we didn't really think about what was happening. We were just dazed.'

In a single day the Russians deported 220,000 Poles, cramming them like cattle into 110 goods trains. In the next four months another two million were deported. For three weeks the packed train steamed on, finally disgorging the bewildered Poles at a frozen forest near Archangel in northern Russia. Men, women and children were set to work as slave labour, felling trees and chopping logs for the Soviet war effort. And then in the autumn of 1941 things changed. Hitler invaded the Soviet Union and the Russians were suddenly allies of the Poles, granting 'amnesty' to their slaves.Hundreds of thousands of Poles crowded back on to the railways. The men, including Stanislaw, went to join the Polish Army being formed in the southern Soviet Union. Women and children headed for resettlement camps in Persia. 'There were so many people dying, so many orphans. In the stations I walked over dead people, not realising what they were. When we arrived at Tehran we were covered with lice and fleas. My mother made a pile of our clothes and burned them.' Within months the Poles were moved on, some to India, others to Africa. Henryka and her mother were taken to a settlement in Uganda ('straw huts but good schools') where they stayed for six years. Then the family was divided for the final time, mother opting to return to Poland, daughter choosing to settle in England. Henryka came to Wolverhampton where she met and married Aleksander Lappo, an officer in the Polish Army.

'What a journey it all was, what a journey,' says Henryka Lappo, smiling sadly as the memories come tumbling back. 'But not a journey I would have wished on anyone.' *February 1990*

The Army's first VC

Jim Miller was born in 1910 and, true to Army tradition, was called Dusty as soon as he enlisted in the Poor Bloody Infantry in 1931. At his home in Leamore, Walsall, Dusty Miller describes his earliest memory, of a Zeppelin raid on Wearside in the First World War. 'Two of our planes attacked it and it burst into two lots of flame. I was holding hands with my mother and we could see the crew jumping out and falling to their death. 'I said, "Ma, look at those poor men," but she said, "They're only Germans."'

It was the age of Empire. By the time he was twenty young Jim had been sent off to Canada to work as a farm-hand. Returning to dirt-poor Britain he did what the Millers had always done; he joined the Durham Light Infantry. Soon he was guarding the jewel in the Imperial crown, India. By 1938 he had served his time and was married and living in Walsall with a baby on the way. Then Hitler invaded Poland and Private Miller was recalled to the colours. In May 1940 he was digging trenches in France, awaiting the Nazi invasion in high spirits. Britain had beaten the Huns in 1918 and would surely do it again. 'We were told the Germans were a load of duffers. Everyone knew their tanks were just cars covered in cardboard.'

And then reality arrived in the form of Stuka dive-bombers. Stuck in a field with a single machine-gun, Dusty Miller tried hopelessly to shoot them down. 'I was firing away and this one went by so low and so close I could see the pilot. He was waving and smiling at me.'

In the days that followed the full might of German blitzkrieg (literally 'lightning war') fell on the Brits. 'They were so well organised. Nothing could stand against them.'

The Durhams fell back. By 15 May they were defending the south side of the river Dyle, east of Brussels. It was a bitter defence, Germans and Brits blazing away at close range. In the midst of it all was a young officer, Dickie Annand. 'I'd only noticed him a couple of times before but he seemed very nice. He was always smiling, a bit like Tony Blair.' Annand raced forward to the top of a ridge, pelting the Germans below with hand grenades. He was wounded but went back again for more grenades. 'I was filling a sandbag with grenades for him and he was slinging them, dozens of them. God Almighty, he killed some Germans.' The officer managed to withdraw his platoon and then, regardless of his own safety, went back alone to rescue his wounded batman in a wheelbarrow.

A few days later, on the road to the coast, Dusty Miller was knocked unconscious when his convoy was bombed. He was kicked awake by a German soldier who then smashed a rock in his face, destroying his sense of smell for ever. He spent the next five years in prisoner of war camps, escaping in the final days of the war and riding to safety in Czechoslovakia on a tank of the victorious Russian Army. Jim Miller came home to Walsall, raised a family with wife Marion and had no further contact with his old regiment until 1969. Then he attended a DLI reunion. He thought he recognised a tall officer in the crowd.

'You mean Captain Annand VC?' said a comrade. And that was the first Dusty Miller knew that the rearguard battle in 1940 had resulted in Dickie Annand being awarded the army's first Victoria Cross of the war. The pair became firm friends, exchanging letters and revisiting the scene of their finest hour. Annand always seemed slightly embarrassed at his award, repeatedly claiming that every member of his platoon deserved a medal. Dickie Annand died on Christmas Eve 2004 aged ninety.

Dusty Miller is still proud of the dogged way his battalion held off the Germans in order for their mates to escape. And he is proud to have been associated with a man who received the ultimate award for gallantry in the face of the enemy. The strange part, says Dusty Miller, is that at the time, as a thirty-year-old private, the action seemed nothing special. 'It was just a battle. We were fighting hard and bullets were flying everywhere. But it seemed like just another battle.' *January 2005*

Dunkirk: six men in a boat

It was the defeat that should never have happened. In the early weeks of 1940 France and Britain had more tanks, guns and soldiers than Nazi Germany. But while Hitler's Panzer divisions were elated with their easy victory in Poland, the Allies were in disarray. On the rare occasions that the British Expeditionary Force counter-attacked, it inflicted heavy casualties. Some French soldiers, too, fought like lions in the final days of the campaign. But in the main France had little stomach for a fight and Britain was not prepared to risk losing its army. In that spirit of resignation the Wolverhampton Territorials of the 1st/6th South Staffordshire Regiment found themselves on the road to Dunkirk in May 1940. They were already demoralised. Trained as infantry, they had reported to their drill halls on 2 September 1939, full of high hopes of winning the war.

'But the powers-that-be had a marvellous idea,' recalls Tom Rutherford of Penn, then a twenty-seven-year-old platoon commander. 'They split us up as Corps troops. Our job was to build trenches.'

War broke upon them with a flurry of shells in the early hours of 10 May. In a chance meeting one of his fellow officers noticed blood seeping from Rutherford's boots. The young officer and his men had just marched 90 miles in three days.

'We got the order to ditch all our transport in the canal. It was all so bizarre. It was nothing like the war films. I remember we were sitting out, having a meal and then there was a sudden bang and Ted Price, the company clerk, had an arm off. Bang, just like that. And then it was all peaceful again.'

Eventually the South Staffs found themselves at Bray Dunes, 5 miles from Dunkirk. Disorder reigned. 'Suddenly we were told to get rid of all the bolts from the anti-tank rifles and throw them in the river to stop them being used by the Germans. The next thing we were told to go in and get them all out again. Then the dive-bombers would come over. The noise was terrible but the bombs they dropped were nothing. They just blew up a bit of sand.'

Unknown to the South Staffs and the rest of the BEF, the newly appointed Prime Minister, Winston Churchill, had ordered Operation Dynamo, the biggest evacuation in military history. It was intended to last forty-eight hours and rescue just a few thousand troops. In the event the evacuation from Dunkirk lasted ten days. To this day no one knows why Hitler's divisions hung back as an entire army slipped away. Scores of destroyers, merchant ships and the immortal six hundred 'little ships' crewed by their private owners plied between Dunkirk and the British coast. Braving German bombs and strafing, the motley fleet rescued 364,628 troops, of whom 224,686 were British and the rest French. Some waded neck-deep to be plucked aboard steamers; others rowed out in dinghies. Churchill, recognising a defeat when he saw it, refused to issue a Dunkirk medal. But, to the amazement of many soldiers, the British people welcomed the homecoming troops as heroes.

France collapsed within three weeks, but in Britain something called the Dunkirk Spirit was born. The transformation was astonishing. Although they never dreamed it at the time the rag-tag army that shivered and flinched on the beaches were paving the way for the destruction of the Third Reich. Four years after salvation at Dunkirk, infinitely better trained and equipped, the South Staffordshire Regiment took part in the D-Day invasion of Normandy. And this time there was no turning back.

For Ernie 'Sonny' Lomas, Dunkirk is a tale of six men in a boat – and not one with a clue how to row. At his Cannock home, the one-time driver with the Royal Army Service Corps recalls the retreat to the coast and the BEF's wholesale destruction of every scrap of equipment that might have fallen into enemy hands. 'It broke your heart, seeing those huge Scammell lorries being set on fire. There were fields full of them, just waiting to be destroyed.'

A twenty-one-year-old volunteer, Mr Lomas saw British troops waiting patiently in the dunes to be called forward into rowing boats. 'There was no panic – all I wanted was to get home.' But as his group set off it became clear no one knew how to row. He jumped over the side to push the boat clear. To this day he treasures his old army service manual, stained red by his driving licence and the Dunkirk salt water.

Taken home on the destroyer HMS *Express*, Mr Lomas went on to serve in two great victories, El Alamein and D-Day. 'I always think Dunkirk was a victory, too. Looking back, it was a wonderful feat even if we didn't think so at the time.'

At his Willenhall home Dunkirk medic Tom Jones remembers his grisly introduction to blitzkrieg. He and a pal were idly looking round a First World War cemetery in Flanders when an aircraft appeared above. 'We were so naïve, we thought bits were falling off it.'

The 'bits' turned out to be bombs. The medics dived for cover in a newly dug grave and the explosions tore the cemetery apart, disinterring the remains of old soldiers.

Ordered back to Dunkirk, they helped to bury the dead in the shell holes of the harbour and assisted a thousand wounded men on to ships. 'From the military point of view it was an absolute shambles, a defeat, a rout. We were pushed into the sea. Why do we make such a fuss of Dunkirk? Because it gave so many of us the chance to get back and have another go.'

Reg Till was a nineteen-year-old gunner at Dunkirk. He recalls: 'From beginning to end it was a balls-up. We hadn't a clue where we were, what we were doing or where we were going. On the road to Dunkirk we were bombed and the civilians were going down like ninepins. I remember jumping out of the truck and cradling a little girl of nine or so. But it was no use, she was mangled.'

Operation Dynamo was a miracle of deliverance. And yet for the demoralised, confused soldiers of the British Expeditionary Force, chased halfway across France by the invading German Army, it was chaos. Mr Till, of Dudley Port, was part of a grandly styled 'flying column', designed to prevent a German breakthrough in northern France. In reality it was a bunch of assorted squaddies with one old field gun, minus its sights, and a 15cwt truck. 'We were like a fire brigade, dashing all over the place. We were told to attack anything on wheels.'

When the shells ran out the lads were ordered to ditch the gun and head for the coast. 'We had a hell of a job trying to find somewhere to dump it. All the ditches for miles were full of dumped equipment. We were formed into columns, slowly shuffling down to the sea. I've no idea what sort of boat it was. They sent us below, gave us coffee and a cheese sandwich and I slept all the way back to Dover.'

The Dunkirk men were astonished to be greeted as heroes. Gunner Till and his pals, still in torn battledress, were sent north to rejoin their unit. 'At Halifax we fell in with some miners. They said, "You from Dunkirk? Come and have a drink, lad."'

Later in the war Reg Till fought in the Italian campaign with mobile anti-tank guns. 'We could knock the turret off a German tank at a thousand yards. But by then we were a different army from the one at Dunkirk. Let's be honest, Dunkirk was a shambles. If it hadn't been for the Navy that would have been the end of it.'

Cecil Rhodes could have missed the Second World War simply by taking a doctor's advice. In 1934, as a twenty-year-old looking for adventure, he tried to join the Territorial Army in Wolverhampton. But the regimental doctor listened to his chest and shook his head. 'This never tells a lie,' said the doctor indicating his stethoscope. 'You've had a serious illness. Go home and look after yourself.'

Turned down by the South Staffordshire Regiment, Cecil promptly applied to the local TA cavalry unit, the Staffordshire Yeomanry, and was accepted. He smiles at a system that judged him unfit for foot-soldiering but fine for charging on horseback. After a year with the Yeomanry he transferred to the South Staffs. All went well until 3 September 1939 when Cecil and his comrades in the South Staffs 6th Battalion were ordered to remove the 'T' insignia from their shoulders. Britain was at war with Germany. The Territorials were part of the Regular Army. Eight months later the battalion was in Belgium as Hitler's finest thundered towards them in a fury of bomb blasts and tank fire. The Black Country lads fell back, marching for their lives. In one break the adjutant Peter Windridge told the private, 'Rhodes, put your steel helmet on or you'll get . . .' The order was drowned out by a huge blast as a German dive-bomber found its target. Cecil was unhurt but the officer fell gravely injured with a head wound. 'He was covered in blood and shaking like a leaf. I gave him a sherry glass-full of whisky. He always said afterwards that it saved his life.'

Dog-tired, Cecil and his thirty-strong company arrived at Dunkirk, clambering over a pile of bodies to reach the beach through a gap in the massive sea wall. 'The funny thing is how quiet it all was. There was a lull and someone took a roll call on the beach.'

Their first attempt to board a rescue boat failed. It was out of diesel. Soaked and dispirited, the Tommies dried out in a cellar. 'The next day the bombing started at 7am and went on until 10pm. Eventually, we were taken off a breakwater by a warship. Someone gave me a bun. We hadn't eaten for so long it tasted as good as a roast chicken.'

But the British Army was in despair. Driven out of France by the German blitzkrieg, it had left thousands of dead, wounded and prisoners behind, and much of its equipment. 'We were all a bit gloomy. We didn't want to talk about it. People were saying it was all over. A lot of the lads thought Jerry would be coming straight over after us. But I think Jerry had probably done more than he planned to do. If the Germans had had some boats they could have come straight over. But they hadn't.'

Back home the rag-tag army was astonished, and ashamed, to be treated as heroes. 'We were sent to London and the Salvation Army took us to a theatre. Someone on stage said there were some lads from Dunkirk in. We stood up and everyone clapped us. But we didn't feel like heroes. We felt we had done our country down. But what else could we do?' *May 1990*

That Spitfire sensation

Britain's legendary wartime leader Winston Churchill summed up the Battle of Britain: 'Never in the field of human conflict was so much owed by so many to so few.' Former Spitfire pilot Joe Doley puts it rather differently: 'We were too young and too daft to know any better,' he grins over a pint of mild at Wolverhampton's United Services Club. He was just twenty when he first got his hands on a Spitfire after months spent training on slow, unexciting Harvards. He remembers the tight fit of the Spitfire cockpit, the cramped headroom and the rattle of the last occupant's rubbish in the Perspex canopy every time he flew upside down. Above all, he recalls the unmistakable roar and brute power of its Merlin engine. The slender lines of the immortal fighter came to symbolise the Battle of Britain. The Spitfire may have looked beautiful, but it was temperamental and notoriously difficult to land, take off and taxi because of the huge blind spot caused by its long nose.

Doley's first, sobering, sight of the 'Spit' was of two machines pitched nose-first into the turf at his training base. 'We were always trained to open the throttle slowly but fully to take off. Well, that Spit, that bloody thing just leaped away. Before you got the wheels up you were over the Irish Sea!'

Joe Doley, of Wolverhampton, was never the archetypal upper-crust pilot. An ordinary painter and decorator, he saved up for pre-war flying lessons at five bob an hour and first flew with the RAF as a sergeant. He remembers his first dogfight as a confused, terrifying affair. 'Some Messerschmitt 109s came over the top of our formation. I just pulled up and shot at them. Everybody was all over the place and I was scared. You just looked at the aircraft, you never thought about who was in it.' His first kill came one morning over the Isle of Wight as two Me 109s suddenly flashed out of the mist. 'One of them turned tail and went for home but eventually I caught him up. I could see my bullets hitting him and suddenly there was this explosion, a big flash on the side of his cockpit. I felt bloody good. You have to remember when you're only twenty you don't really think. Maybe some of the old chaps, say twenty-seven or so, had started to think properly, but we hadn't. You're just exhilarated. The only guilt you feel is when you're burying your own chaps.' The Battle of Britain that raged overhead as young Joe Doley was in training was the prelude to Hitler's planned invasion of England, Operation Sealion. Channel ports were clogged with invasion barges and plans were made for landings along the south coast. But Goering's Luftwaffe first had to win control of the skies. The Battle of Britain began in July with dive-bomb attacks on British convoys in the Channel, and in August the Luftwaffe shifted its attention to the destruction of Fighter Command.

It was a desperate time. With airfields bombed and fighter aircraft either wrecked on the ground or shot down, the RAF was running short not only of planes but of pilots. Goering declared that Tuesday 13 August would be Adlertag (Eagle Day), marking the final sweeping of the RAF from the skies. The Luftwaffe launched 1,485 sorties but lost forty-five aircraft to the RAF's thirteen.

On 15 August came even greater air battles, the RAF losing forty-two fighters but destroying ninety enemy machines. On 31 August the airfields at Biggin Hill, Lympne, Manston and Hawkinge were bombed out of action. On that grim day the RAF lost thirty-eight planes. But deliverance was at hand. On 24 August, apparently by accident, German Heinkels bombed London. The next night eighty-one British bombers attacked Berlin, to the fury of Hitler. On 7 September Goering switched his attacks from airfields to the capital. London's agony was Britain's salvation as the RAF gathered its strength. On Sunday 15 September hundreds of Spitfires and Hurricanes greeted German bomber crews who had been told the RAF was down to a handful of planes. Sixty German planes were shot down for the loss of twenty-nine British. On that day the RAF claimed victory in the Battle of Britain. Two days later Hitler ordered the indefinite postponement of Operation Sealion. By failing to knock out Britain before attacking Russia, Hitler made the elementary mistake of fighting a war on two fronts.

Joe Doley missed the Battle of Britain, not flying operationally until the end of 1940. But he flew with veterans of the battle and remembers the spirit of the dark days and the top brass at his training base 'getting a real panic on' over the threat of fifth columnists. His strongest memories are not of aerial combat but of the constant, senseless deaths of friends in accidents. He recalls a Spitfire flight 'beating up' their airfield at 200 feet in sheer exuberance at having shot down a number of enemy fighters. Two wingtips touched, two Spitfires crashed, two more of the 'Few' had perished.Above all, he remembers Jock, the young Scots pilot killed in the mid-air collision of two RAF aircraft on the day before the war ended.

Historians may turn the 'Few' into heroes, but Joe Doley remembers a bunch of ordinary men who were simply too young and too naïve to understand anything other than the daily requirement to climb 5 miles high in tiny fighters and go wherever they were directed. At twenty -two he was selected to become an officer. In the huddle outside the commissioning board, those waiting to go in for their interview quizzed those who had come out. 'They want to know things like who's the Prime Minister,' said one shocked candidate.

'Well, who is the Prime Minister?' asked the others.

'And they want to know who's in charge of the Eighth Army.'

'Well, who is in charge?'

After much debate Warrant Officer 754184 Doley decided on Churchill and Montgomery. And with that grip on world affairs he was duly commissioned, serving with the RAF in Spitfires, Hurricanes and Mustangs until 1947. 'Ah, those days! I wouldn't have done without them. If I had my time again I'd do it all again, and a lot more, too. And if there was a Spit outside here now I know I could start it up and taxi it. Could I fly it again? I don't know. You know, I might just try.'
September 1990

Radar tips the balance

It was 1940. Hitler's stormtroopers were just across the Channel. At a top-secret establishment in Suffolk the plan, in case of invasion, was to evacuate the women on lorries and destroy all the equipment with hand grenades. The secret code for this last-ditch act was three rings on the field telephone. One day the three rings sounded. Bernard Blakemore recalls the moment: 'After a while someone said we'd better answer it. It turned out to be someone saying the tea trolley was on its way.' He laughs, recalling the funnier side of Britain's Finest Hour.

It all began for him with the fastest week in his life. On 3 September 1939 Bernard Blakemore, a young team leader at the BBC's mighty Empire station at Daventry, was ordered to get every transmitter running on full power for an important announcement. A few hours later Prime Minister Neville Chamberlain broadcast his grim message that Britain was at war with Germany. The next day young Blakemore was released for war service by the BBC. Two days later he arrived at Bawdsey Manor, a remote country house on the Suffolk coast. Today the name may mean nothing, but in the darkest days of the last war the brainpower assembled at Bawdsey was paving the way to victory, thanks to a great British secret.

Unlike some at the establishment, Bernard was not overawed by a mansion. He grew up in a prosperous Wolverhampton family and married Maria, daughter of Alderman Frank Myatt, a wealthy Mayor of Wolverhampton. He recalls an idyllic early life of grand balls and parties among the affluent middle class of the Black Country. What impressed him at Bawdsey was not so much the surroundings as the mission. 'The first thing that happened,' he recalls at his comfortable Tettenhall home, 'was that the Commanding Officer called four of us into his office. He said that what he was about to tell us must go no further, and that no-one must know what we were doing.'

At the age of twenty-two Bernard was then told the big secret. It was an invention called RDF, Radio Direction Finding, later to be known as radar. It originated in the 1930s when the War Office asked scientists whether it might be possible to build a 'death ray' to knock out enemy pilots. The answer, from one of Britain's top radio experts, Robert Watson Watt, was that death rays were a non-starter, but it might be possible to detect enemy aircraft by bouncing radio waves off them. A few shaky experiments in 1935 persuaded a dubious Whitehall to invest in radar. Great brains in electronics were assembled in the serene grounds of Bawdsey.Bernard Blakemore, commissioned into the RAF, became part of the team that perfected radar and built the connections between radar stations and RAF airfields. In the summer of 1940 this combination of early warning and brave pilots brought victory in the Battle of Britain. 'I would never want to diminish the courage of our RAF pilots. But when they came back from missions they always said they could not have done it without being put in the right place at the right time.'

On 16 August 1940 Hitler predicted that England would be invaded in a matter of weeks. But time after time his bombers were ambushed 5 miles high by Spitfire and Hurricanes which, thanks to Bawdsey, always knew they were coming. Barely a month after his proud boast Hitler postponed the invasion indefinitely.

'Bawdsey was a magical sort of place,' recalls Bernard Blakemore. 'No-one who worked there will ever forget it. It is such an important part of our history.' *July 2004*

The Hawker Hurricane

Bob Lickley was born to fix things. He came from a long line of engineers and by 1937 was in Wolverhampton working on one of the most exciting projects of the age. At Bean's factory he was one of twenty apprentice lads preparing Thunderbolt, the British contender for the world land-speed record. There was a chance for some of the lads to go to the United States for the record attempt by Captain George Eyston, but Bob's father, a dour Scot, had other ideas. 'He told me that racing cars was no part of my education. So I decided to stand up to him and do something about it.'

Young Bob set off from the family home in Shropshire, and at the age of seventeen years and two months signed up in Birmingham as an aero-engine fitter with the Royal Air Force. By the long, hot summer of 1940 he was with 56 Squadron based at North Weald in Essex, in the front line of the Battle of Britain. The squadron motto is *Quid si coelum ruat?* – What if heaven falls? At times it seemed it might. France had surrendered. Britain stood alone. Hitler's invasion barges were massing across the Channel. Once the German Luftwaffe had knocked out the RAF the Nazi invasion could begin. For a few tense and bloody weeks the future of the world hung on a few hundred RAF fighter pilots and their ground crews, some still in their teens.

'We were just kids,' smiles Bob Lickley of Albrighton as the years slip away and the memories of 1940 flood back. He recalls the thrill, after training on biplanes, of seeing his first Hawker Hurricanes. 'We just lived in awe of the things,' he says. 'Although I had been an engineer since I was a young chap, this was such a colossal piece of equipment and so complex.'

Hurricanes equipped more squadrons, scored more 'kills' and brought more wounded pilots safely home than any other RAF fighter. And yet then, as now, the Hurricane was overshadowed by the glamorous Supermarine Spitfire. 'I suppose it was inevitable. The Spitfire was faster and more manoeuvrable and, let's face it, much more graceful. But the Hurricane was a wonderful plane and a lot easier to repair. They would come back covered in bullet holes. But because they were covered in fabric rather than steel, we would stick on these little red circular patches and a coat of cellulose dope. When there wasn't enough time to paint them they'd fly off covered in these red patches.' Bob's mood changes. He remembers the pilots – 'just lads like the rest of us' – who never came back. How did these fresh-faced warriors cope with the threat of death by bullet or burns 5 miles high, sometimes three or four times a day? 'They had a whole range of attitudes. Some of them became all religious and believed nothing could happen to them. Others said, to hell with it all, we might be dead tomorrow. When you have lived and worked with these people, even if only for a couple of months, you became very, very close to them. And when they didn't come back you missed them dreadfully. Sometimes it was ages before we knew if they were dead or not.'

All summer the Luftwaffe battered the RAF airfields; 56 Squadron had to relocate after North Weald was bombed. But somehow, miraculously, there were always just enough pilots, planes and ground crew to keep the waves of German bombers at bay. The Battle of Britain lasted from 10 July until 15 September 1940. The RAF lost about 650 aircraft, the Luftwaffe about 1,100. But while German aircrew were invariably killed or captured, RAF pilots in damaged planes could crash-land or parachute and be quickly back in action. Unable to dominate the skies, Hitler abandoned his plan to invade Britain.

Young Sgt Lickley left 56 Squadron for an extraordinary war overseas, which took him to South Africa, Egypt, Palestine, Syria and Africa. A member of the RAF Association and 56 Sqn Association, he is painfully aware that he is a dying breed. Back in 1940 the lads who swept the summer skies clear of Nazi intruders were known as 'The Few'. They are desperately few today.And that is why, with all due respect to the Spitfire, Bob Lickley speaks up for the Hurricane. *March 2006*

The doomed Greek campaign

In 1939 Tony Southall was a dashing young trooper with the Inns of Court Yeomanry, one of London's smartest TA cavalry units. Recruited exclusively from lawyers and nicknamed 'The Devil's Own', they cut a dash riding through London on horses borrowed from the Life Guards. But a few months later the horses had passed into history. In April 1941 Tony Southall was watching his machine-gun bullets bounce off German tanks in the doomed Greek campaign. British troops had been rushed from North Africa to help the Greeks in their war against the Italians and Germans. It ended in disaster. Captured at the port of Kalamata, the British were marched into captivity. Those who fell by the wayside were shot.

'I knew I couldn't go on. I just sat down at the side of the road and said 'go on – shoot me'. And suddenly this German officer behind shouted 'Oxford!' I hadn't a clue what was going on.'

It turned out that the German had studied at Oxford University before the war and had happy memories of England. He put the exhausted Englishman in a captured lorry, an act of mercy that certainly saved his life. Tony Southall spent the next four years as a prisoner of war in a succession of camps. When he came home, weighing just seven stone, he went on to become a successful solicitor in Wolverhampton.

At eighty-two he published a remarkable memoir, including an account of a mass breakout of twenty-seven POWs from Warburg camp. He also recalled witnessing massed Allied air raids on German towns. 'I don't think we felt any sympathy for them.' *March 2005*

Valour at sea

Dave Everett of Penn, Wolverhampton, was torpedoed and sunk in the Atlantic in 1941. He witnessed the astonishing heroism of a Midland padre – and later met an unlikely convert to Catholicism. It is one of those extraordinary war stories that proves fact can be stranger than fiction.

'Our troopship SS *Anselm* left Glasgow escorted by the destroyer *Challenger*. I remember scanning the bulletin board six days later. It said: "For the attention of all servicemen. Pyjamas can be worn now that we are out of the danger area." A matelot with a stiff beard behind me growled, "That must have been written by a U-boat commander. Is there a safe place anywhere in the Atlantic?"

'My pal Andy and I were both in the boxing team at our last station and to keep ourselves in trim we were up at 5am trotting around the deck. Saturday morning, 5 July, was no exception. We had just completed one circuit when the torpedo struck. From then on it was a nightmare. The alarm sounded. By instinct we headed for the lifeboat station. I witnessed chaos and panic beyond anything I could imagine. Despair and hopelessness was written in everybody's face. I heard screams and howls from guys trapped down below. I watched guys fighting with each other, seemingly for no reason at all. The destroyer *Challenger* had nosed in towards the back of the ship, catching servicemen dropping from the stern.

'Padre Pugh, the first padre at the RAF Bridgnorth station, was haggling with a couple of erks [aircraftmen] to lower him down so that he could bring solace to the doomed erks trapped below. His last words were, "My love of God is greater than my fear of death". The ship went down within twenty minutes. The reports of casualties ranged from 250 to over 400. Someone, somewhere made a cock-up with their sums. Later I read that Padre Pugh had been awarded the George Cross posthumously for his bravery.'

There is a curious footnote. Dave Everett recalls: 'Years afterwards I met another survivor who had converted to Catholicism, having witnessed this RC priest sacrificing his life. The irony was that it was a mistake. Padre Pugh was C of E. But he shared a cabin with a Catholic priest. In the pandemonium each had donned the wrong tunic.' *December 1999*

The Rev Herbert Cecil Pugh (1898–1941) was awarded the George Cross posthumously in April 1947. The official citation says he was last seen 'kneeling with the men in prayer as the ship sank'.

From Hong Kong to Kobe House
At the annual Kobe House reunions they enjoy a good sing-song. But there's one Second World War classic that is never heard. By general agreement *Roll Out the Barrel* is banned. It just wouldn't be right. To the old soldiers who survived the hell hole of Kobe House prisoner of war camp, barrels have a special significance. There was a stock of old barrels at Kobe. As the POWs steadily wasted away and died, the Japanese ordered the barrels to be used as coffins. 'They were small, about the size of apple barrels,' recalls Jack Bowen at his home in Bedford Road, West Bromwich. 'You can imagine how it was, trying to put a six-foot bloke into a little barrel like that. We had to get them into a crouching position; we had to break their bones. It all happened in front of the blokes in the sick bay and, of course, they were wondering if they would be next. It was very depressing. I remember helping to lift one Signals chap after he died. He weighed 47 pounds, just a skeleton. It was horrible, horrible. That's the sort of thing you never forget.'

Kobe House was a disused warehouse, pressed into service to accommodate Allied POWs like Jack Bowen, a Lance-Sergeant who had served in a Royal Artillery fort in Hong Kong. The colony fell to the Japanese on Christmas Day 1941. Surrender came as a surprise. 'Someone pushed a bottle of whisky in my hand and said it was all over. I couldn't believe it. I thought we were winning; a lot of us did.'

After a spell in a POW pen in Kowloon, the British were loaded on to the freighter *Lisbon Maru*. It was torpedoed and more than a thousand POWs drowned. Mr Bowen was among nine hundred who were rounded up from a chain of islands and shipped on to Kobe. To Emperor Hirohito's warriors, a foe that surrendered was beneath contempt and deserved little mercy. Between 1941 and 1945, when the war ended, 27,000 British POWs died in Japanese camps. 'In the first month, a hundred of us died simply for want of the stuff to keep us alive. There were no medicines. They just wasted away from beri-beri, diphtheria, dysentery and malnutrition.'

Those who survived became accustomed to the routine bestiality of Japanese soldiers. 'Some of the men were really badly beaten up, I mean boots and rifle butts, just for tossing coins. We didn't have an interpreter and we didn't understand that putting your thumb on the image of Hirohito was an insult. One chap was beaten so badly that his arm was broken because he didn't bow quickly enough to the camp paymaster.'

Forty-odd years after the nightmare of Kobe House, the former Gunner draws a clear line between the general wickedness of war and the evil of those who engineer war. 'In war, there are a lot of war crimes on the winning side that never come up, like our bombing of Dresden. There is a new generation. I would hate it if the Japanese blamed my grandchildren for my misdeeds. But Hirohito was the Commander-in-Chief. He knew what was going on, there is no question about it. He also knew that the date had been set for the execution of all us prisoners of war if the Japanese mainland was invaded. I have no doubt that the order would have been carried out.' *January 1989*

Hurricanes over Murmansk

Eric 'Ginger' Carter was a sergeant pilot in an almost-forgotten theatre of war. For a few hectic months in 1941 he was one of a handful of British pilots fighting for the Russians.

'When people hear we were fighting for the Russians, they assume we were a bunch of Communists, like something out of the Spanish Civil War,' he smiles over coffee at his home in Chaddesley Corbett, near Kidderminster, where he lives with his wife, Phyllis. It wasn't like that. When the war began in 1939 Russia was an ally of Hitler's Germany. But in June 1941 Hitler launched his ill-fated invasion of Russia. In one of his finest speeches, Churchill, who hated Communism, launched a new crusade, to protect the Russian people from 'the brutish masses of the Hun soldiery'. The nation responded, and Britain eventually supplied Russia with monthly deliveries of 1,000 tanks, 2,000 armoured cars and hundreds of guns. A total of 3,600 warplanes were dispatched. The first gesture was the sending of two RAF squadrons, 81 and 134, to protect the vital ice-free port of Murmansk. Thus, as the winter of 1941 approached, Eric Carter, a twenty-year-old Hurricane pilot, found himself on a remote aerodrome on the Arctic Circle with primitive sanitation, surrounded by peasant Russians 'who would cut your throat as soon as look at you' and the certain knowledge that one mistake in the air spelled death. 'If you came down there was never a chance of getting back. It was like the North Pole out there. They say that youngsters grow up more quickly these days but, honestly, if we had gone into action like some of the youth of today, we wouldn't have lasted a fortnight. You grew up very fast; three months was a hell of a long time. You could live your whole life in forty-five minutes.'

The Hurricanes notched up an incredible rate of 'kills' over Murmansk, shooting down fifteen German warplanes for the loss of just one British plane. 'You can cope with death better at that age. You couldn't afford to think about it too much. If you did, it would drive you round the bend. But if you love your country you should be prepared to fight and die for it.'

Young Sergeant Carter was at first horrified at the Russians' attitude to total war. 'Life was very cheap. Some of their men would get drunk at night, collapse on the airfield and freeze to death. They'd simply sling them on a truck the next morning. No-one seemed to know who they were; there was never any sort of roll-call.' But the marvellous will to fight of his new allies made a lasting impression. And the Russians never forgot the Hurricane pilots. Four of them became the only British citizens to receive the coveted Order of Lenin from the Soviets. To mark the fortieth anniversary of the end of the war, 'Ginger' Carter and his old comrade Ibby Waud were presented with gold medals at the Soviet Embassy. 'The Russians are very patriotic. We have a generation coming up who you're almost embarrassed to tell that you've been listening to the ceremony at the Cenotaph. The Russians, on the other hand, seem to be very much behind the Motherland. Sometimes I can't believe it was all so long ago. I feel sure if I got back in a Hurricane after a couple of hours' instruction I'd be able to fly it again. It was a wonderful old aircraft; you really became a part of it.' *June 1987*

Life as a Japanese POW

It is the heads he cannot forget. Imagine a newly built road like the Birmingham New Road at Tipton, says Bill Wheale, with saplings planted every few yards. Every sapling on the road he remembers near Singapore was protected by an ornate tube of spiked railings. On top of each railing was a freshly severed human head. Buzzing around every sapling was a stinking black cloud of flies. When the Japanese conquered Singapore in February 1942 more than 130,000 British and Allied soldiers were captured. In the following three years thousands perished through disease, malnutrition, beatings and casual execution. As Bill Wheale's unit, the 4th Battalion of the Suffolk Regiment, was marched off into captivity, the Japanese treatment of local civilians was a shocking foretaste of things to come. In his comfortable home in Tipton the big old soldier recalls how the locals risked everything to toss a handful of food or a few cigarettes to the dejected British squaddies. If they were spotted, retribution by bayonet and Samurai sword was terrible. 'You'd see a bloke enjoying a fag and know that, a mile or so down the road, some poor little kiddie of four or five had his head chopped off for it.'

He was marched inland to work on the infamous Burma Railway, a military supply route for the bloodily expanding Japanese empire. Of the three thousand who set out in his group only 115 survived the war. Bill Wheale does not dwell on the inhumanity of his captors. How does it feel to see your own mates lined up and killed by firing squad for trying to escape? 'It feels bad' is all he says. The worst bits he has banished to the back of his mind.

We chat for two hours, and most of his memories are of food, or the lack of it. 'We had a little rice. It was rotten and there were maggots galore. If you threw the maggots away you wouldn't have much rice left. I ate my own boots. You'd cut the sole into small pieces, chew it at night and save it for the next night. The best taste of all was the polish.'

Once he took a swipe at a guard. He was beaten half to death and sentenced to be shot. 'When you're whipped the bugs and butterflies go creeping all over you. You almost want another beating to get rid of them.'

He was spared execution when a Japanese officer, filthy from jungle fighting, arrived and demanded a haircut. Bill Wheale had a worn-out old kitchen knife. He still has it. 'I nearly scalped the bugger,' he grins with satisfaction. 'But he seemed very happy with it and gave me cigarettes and a pineapple.'

After cholera hit the prison camp, he had to bury scores of his comrades. 'That was the hardest part. As soon as you got the symptoms even our own lads didn't want us. We were like lepers.'

As a cholera suspect, Bill Wheale was put to work burying the dead. In one fortnight his sickly, half-starved squad was burying forty corpses a day. He survived that ordeal, and another even more frightful, when his right leg became so ulcerated that amputation seemed inevitable. His mates scrounged a handful of toilet-disinfectant crystals. The camp doctor scraped the ulcer away to the bone and covered the cavity with the crystals. When the wound went septic a handful of maggots was applied to digest the pus and did 'a wonderful job'. One way or another, as food or wound-cleaners, maggots helped him survive. But it was a close-run thing. As a fit, athletic twenty-one-year-old, Bill weighed 11 stone when he was captured. By the time it was all over, he was a pitiful 6 stone 12 pounds. After three years of cholera, beri-beri, ulcers, beatings, hard labour and too many deaths to remember, Bill Wheale's war ended bizarrely. He was part of a ragged, skeletal working party in a high mountain valley in Burma. Suddenly, on the other side of the valley, angel-white against the jungle greenery, was a figure yelling, 'You're free!'

'We thought he was a nutter. He turned out to be from a British submarine. He had seen our smoke and come to investigate. It was 29 August 1945. The war had been over since 15 August.'

Bill will never forget his first meal after being rescued: 'I ate twenty-seven rounds of bread and butter and five courses of every meal.' *April 1999*

Lessons from El Alamein

If anyone understands how the ground soldiers feel now (during the 1991 Gulf War), it is Neville Warner. In November 1942 he was one of the first Desert Rats, a twenty-two-year-old Sherman tank driver serving with the Warwickshire Yeomanry in North Africa. The epic battle of El Alamein had become bogged down in German minefields covered by the feared 88mm guns. The Yeomanry was part of 9th Armoured Brigade, whose job, in Operation Supercharge, was to get the battle moving. The Eighth Army commander, General Montgomery, told the brigade to expect 90 per cent casualties. He was proved right. Delayed by minefields, the brigade's Shermans, Grants and Crusaders were framed by the rising sun and picked off like targets in a fairground. Of more than 150 tanks sent into battle only seven survived.Neville Warner of Stratford-upon-Avon, was the driver of one of them. His thoughts today are with the lads in the Gulf, preparing to assault Iraqi positions in their Challenger tanks and Warrior armoured vehicles. 'Fighting in tanks was hot, dirty, sandy and very frightening,' he recalls. 'The first thing we learned was to keep moving. Stand still and they'd hit you. We were supposed to close the hatch but we kept it open so that if we were hit we could get out. The drivers all wore gym shoes because the heels of your boots caught on the escape hatches. In combat the rule book was the first thing to go over the side.'

With black wartime humour, the Sherman was known to its crews as the Ronson, because it easily caught fire when hit. 'If you took a direct hit the question wasn't whether it would go up, but when. When the 88s opened up, we could see tanks going up all around us. It was a strange feeling. Time loses all meaning when you go into battle. You feel a sort of elation, an easy-come, easy-go sort of attitude.'

His own tank took two hits, mercifully only glancing blows which damaged the tracks and put the Sherman out of action for a couple of hours. But after Operation Supercharge, the dreadful scale of the casualties was obvious. How do young men cope with such things? 'Because battles tend to ebb and flow, it could be two or three days before you knew who had been killed. It hits you hard when they're your own friends. But if they're other people, well, it may sound hard, but you just get on with it. There are so many things to do.' Today, in spirit, Neville is with the tank crews in the Gulf. 'Of course we should be there. Why the hell did we mess about so long? It was obvious to anyone with any knowledge of the Middle East that if Saddam Hussein had carried on Jordan would have fallen to him in a few months, and then it would have been Saudi Arabia, Yemen, Egypt. The whole region would have been in turmoil.' Has he any tips for today's Desert Rats? 'Things have changed too much. The worst that could hit us was the 88. Today they can hit you from 20 miles away. The best tip is just to keep moving.' *January 1991*

Christmas Day on the convoys

Four days out, and homeward bound from Canada, something strange appeared on the radar of the ageing destroyer HMS *Winchelsea*.

'The shadow was appearing and then disappearing,' recalls Bob Lilley. His home in Castlecroft, Wolverhampton, is a world away from the freezing North Atlantic and the daily terrors of wartime convoy duty. 'We thought it might be a sub on the surface. The Old Man ordered us to run it down.'

But as HMS *Winchelsea*, a veteran of the First World War, swung into action, the object came into view. Not a German U-boat but a ship's lifeboat with one small sail taking her, with infinite slowness, on a westward course. Leading Seaman Lilley was ordered to take command of the destroyer's cutter. With a team of men he ploughed through the calm grey sea toward the lifeboat. The sight that greeted him still haunts him. In the lifeboat were ten British merchant seamen. They were dead and frozen stiff, and the seagulls had taken their eyes. Their vessel, probably a freighter, had been attacked by U-boats some days before. These doomed sailors had been given no time to take to the boats. 'Two of them were wearing only vests. They had obviously come straight out of the engine room.'

Adrift in the Atlantic in December, hundreds of miles from the Canadian coast, the sailors could only raise their pitiful sail, huddle together for warmth and hope for a rescue that never came. They perished along with more than 29,000 others of the British Merchant Navy in the six-year struggle to keep Britain supplied with food and munitions for the fight against Nazism. Their vanished freighter was one of 2,246 merchant ships lost. Back then, with the ever-present threat of U-boats, there was no time to reflect on their heroism. *Winchelsea*'s cutter returned to the destroyer with the lifeboat in tow. The ten frozen bodies were lifted gently aboard.

Leading Seaman Lilley had joined the Royal Navy in 1938, the year the war started. He had seen too many bodies to be shocked. But the sadness stays with him. 'The next day we buried them at sea.' Bob Lilley had a great collection of photographs of his ship and the shipmates he served with through the darkest days of the Battle of the Atlantic. Then his house was burgled and the intruders stole the lot. 'I'm a very disillusioned man. I often wonder if it was all worthwhile.'

And try as he might, even after all these years, he cannot shake off the memory of that lifeboat with its crew of ten dead men. How could he when it happened on a day usually associated with joy? Bob Lilley was a veteran with three years' service when he was ordered to intercept the drifting lifeboat. Yet he was just a boy of nineteen, a teenager in arms doing his duty – on Christmas Day 1942. *December 2007*

The Bevin Boys

They were as neat as a line of carrots, all spruced up in blazers and flannels, grey hair brushed hard, badges and ties proclaiming them to be Bevin Boys. They thronged the conference centre at Walsall's Bescot Stadium for their annual reunion, swapping memories, remembering the experiences that bind them together, and trying not to get too bitter at the way history has treated them. Then, and even today, the £3-a-week conscript miners had to put up with claims that they were dodging front-line service. Not so. Although about half volunteered for the mines, the rest were simply unlucky. In 1943, faced with eighty thousand miners deserting the pits for military service, the wartime Minister of Labour, Ernest Bevin, launched a series of fortnightly ballots. If your number ended with the chosen digit you were directed into the mines.For some it was a bizarre result. Seventy-two-year-old Warwick Taylor, author of *The Forgotten Conscript* and vice-president of the Bevin Boys Association, spent more than three years in the Air Training Corps, studying to be a radio operator in the RAF. 'But my number was drawn and I had no choice,' he recalls. He was a Bevin Boy for eighteen months before his appeal was successful and he was transferred to the RAF.

Mining was a mixed experience. For some, like Phil Yates, it meant a warm welcome by the pitmen of Yorkshire. Their accents were so broad that he could hardly understand them. 'I had been working in a solicitor's office. Imagine going from that to hard manual work. They were wonderful people, the salt of the earth. They welcomed us into their homes, to eat with them. I still remember the Yorkshire puddings.' When he returned to his native Winchester he recalls, smiling broadly, his own folk could hardly understand him. 'I can still do the Yorkshire lingo now, all those thees and thous.'For Warwick Taylor, also from Winchester and dumped at a deep mine in a tight-knit South Wales village, it was a depressing and isolating experience. 'The attitude towards us was very hostile. They spoke a different language and they seemed to think we were coming to take jobs away from their kith and kin who were away with the armed forces. They'd say things in the street like "go home, why don't you?"'Some experiences were shared by all Bevin Boys, including the horror of having your helmet lamp go out and being alone in the unimaginable blackness of an unlit pit. 'I was a pit-pony driver at the coal face,' recalls Phil Yates, 'and it happened to me three or four times. You could not believe the darkness. All you could do was hold on to the pony because he knew his way back to the pit bottom where the stables were.' And no Bevin Boy will ever forget the 'initiation drop' when instead of going down in the men's cage they would drop at 70 feet per second in the cage used to bring up the coal. For Warwick Taylor, that meant the ear-splitting agony and nose-bleed that goes with virtually falling 3,000 feet.

When the war ended in 1945 no-one seemed to know what to do with the forty-eight thousand Bevin Boys who had dug so much coal and contributed so much towards winning the war. 'I got my call-up only a month before VE Day and I thought, what the hell am I doing here in peacetime?' says Phil Yates. 'When are we going to get demobilised?' Eventually, they were released at the same time as their contemporaries in the armed forces.

By 1948 this curious experiment in turning clerks and schoolboys into miners was over. There was no gratuity, no demob suit, no medal. Soon all the Bevin Boy records were destroyed. To this day no-one knows how many of them perished in the pits. 'There's a lot of bitterness,' says Phil Yates. 'They say we weren't part of the armed forces but, dammit, we were in a way.' *October 1998*

Shot down in Holland

A terrible dilemma of war. Adrian Ammerlaan was a nineteen-year-old working on the family farm in Holland when a neighbour ran up to him. 'You speak English?' he asked.

'Well, school English,' replied the teenager.

'Come quickly. I think there is an Englishman in my tomatoes.' The Englishman turned out to be an RAF pilot shot down during an air raid. He called himself Eddie. He said he came from Birmingham.

'He was only about my age and he was terrified,' Mr Ammerlaan recalls at his home in Castlecroft, Wolverhampton. 'In fact, we were both terrified.'

For this was Nazi-occupied Holland in May 1943, three years after the Germans invaded. Young Adrian had watched the 1940 onslaught as Luftwaffe bombers laid Rotterdam waste and German paratroopers landed on the farm. 'They were evil, brutal bastards. They just took whatever they wanted.'

By 1943 the Nazi occupiers of Holland were regularly using decoys dressed in RAF uniform to trap members of the Dutch Resistance. One false step could lead to the firing squad. So was the young man in flying gear the real thing or part of a trap?

Adrian asked for some sort of proof. From the pocket of his flying jacket the RAF man pulled a Midland Red bus ticket issued the previous day. He was genuine. But what to do for the best? Turning the pilot over to the Germans would have been the safest option, but in a matter of moments the Dutch teenager decided to put his life on the line. Adrian went home and collected some clothes and a pair of clogs before coolly escorting the disguised RAF pilot past search parties of German troops. For the next six weeks Eddie blended into the background, just another worker on the Ammerlaan farm near Delft. And then the worst happened. In Nazi-occupied Europe betrayal was commonplace.

'Someone squealed. Someone must have talked because suddenly the Germans were all over the village. Eddie was quickly captured. I have no idea what happened to him. I never saw him again. But he was in civilian clothes, so he was probably shot.'

Revenge against the Dutch was swift and savage. The Germans used the incident to deport Dutch civilians as slave labour. Every young man in the area was rounded up and loaded on to cattle wagons marked 'Labour Special'. 'I thought it was all over. I thought I would never see home again.'

After a couple of terrible nights in a concentration camp the terrified young Dutch men were unloaded at a German munitions factory close to the Swiss border. They were put to work making everything from bayonets to surgical instruments. But even in the heart of Hitler's Reich, Adrian and his pals found ways to fight the hated enemy. 'Years before, this German soldier had shown me how to dismantle his machine-gun and remove the firing pin.' When Adrian found a consignment of machine-guns destined for the Eastern Front in Odessa he sabotaged them, removing every firing pin.

His escape from Germany into neutral Switzerland was the stuff of movies. After less than three weeks at the factory he and some others got false papers from a talented forger and were taken by train to a station on the border. Here, they slipped into a forest. Soon, German troops with hounds were on their trail. 'This terrible thunderstorm started and the Germans gave up,' he recalls. 'That's what saved us.' Their guide turned back to help another party but was blown to pieces. For the first time the escapees realised they were in a minefield.

At midnight they reached a farmhouse and woke the occupants, steeling themselves to ask the fateful question, 'Ist ihr Schweiz?' (Is this Switzerland?) 'Jawohl, ihr Schweiz,' replied a voice in the dark. For the first time in his tale the old man is moved to tears. His eyes sparkle as he recalls the hospitality shown by the Swiss.

After months working on Swiss farms, Adrian joined a party of volunteers from Holland in the Free Dutch Army. By the winter of 1944 he was a trained soldier, part of a Dutch unit attached to an American division in the Ardennes. In December the Germans launched their last desperate offensive of the war, the Battle of the Bulge. 'I had never been under fire before. The Germans bombarded us and I was surrounded by dead bodies. I was wounded and alone, and I thought if the Germans caught me and found out who I was, well, it wouldn't be good. They were forming up for an attack so I just kept rattling away with my machine-gun. I had lost a lot of blood and then suddenly I heard bagpipes.' The pipes of a Scottish-Canadian unit signalled the arrival of a relief column. 'To this day I still love the sound of bagpipes at the New Year. To me, they are like the trumpets of angels.'

His left leg patched up, Adrian was evacuated to England. In the New Year of 1945 he arrived at the Dutch Army's Princess Irene Brigade based at Wrottesley, Wolverhampton. While he had been decorated for gallantry by the Dutch Queen Wilhelmina and welcomed as a war hero in Britain, he could not return to his home village in Holland. Adrian's decision to help the RAF pilot had brought catastrophe to the settlement. 'So many had lost sons or been marked for life by what had happened. They blamed me, and I can understand it. But how could I have squealed on that poor RAF man? We heard all the time on the BBC that the RAF needed every pilot it could get back.' *January 2006*

The Yanks are coming
If this grass could whisper, what tales it would tell. Of life and love, of tears and death and of homecomings fit for heroes. Today this little patch of England is a caravan site and football pitch. But for two astonishing years in the Second World War it echoed to the sobs, prayers and laughter of thousands of Americans.It was Wolverley Camp, near Kidderminster, home of the 'Fightin' Fifty-Second' General Hospital of the United States Army. Here, hundreds of doctors, nurses and assistants from far-off Syracuse in New York patched up the minds and bodies of American boys wounded in the battlefields of Europe. Four-star generals and politicians passed this way. Bob Hope entertained the camp with a laugh-a-second open-air comedy show. 'Sometimes my wife Lynn and I walk over this place,' says Mike Webster, 'and both of us think we can sense the presence.'All that remains is the old entertainment block. The wards where twenty thousand in-patients and perhaps a hundred thousand outpatients were treated have long gone. As memories faded, there was always the danger that Wolverley's part in the greatest conflict of all time might be forgotten. Mike Webster decided that must not happen. So, despite heart disease, he worked tirelessly to gather information and images of the 52nd General Hospital and erect a suitable memorial, setting up a website and giving many talks on the subject to local groups.

Mike tells how the massive camp was built in a matter of weeks in 1942 and opened in 1943 as the 52nd General Hospital for the American

Army. The hospital was created in Syracuse, New York, and transferred to Wolverley to treat American troops injured in the European theatre of operations. Wolverley was the US Army's main holding centre for a miracle drug that brought terribly wounded and infected patients back from the brink of death. It was penicillin, the first antibiotic. As the wounded began to arrive, first from the Yanks' bloody baptism of fire in North Africa and then from the Normandy campaign, the new drug lived up to its reputation. According to hospital records, of the scores of thousands who passed through Wolverley only four soldiers died of their wounds. The rest were either returned to the front or sent home to their families, proudly wearing the Purple Heart medal for those wounded in action.The Fightin' 52nd was one of a string of US hospitals created across Britain designed to cope with up to ninety thousand battlefield casualties at any one time. As Mike Webster researched, he was awed by the scale of the operation. 'It was total war. Money seemed no object. It was built by British workers and it went up very quickly.' When the war ended in 1945 the Fightin' 52nd packed their bags and returned to New York. But the Wolverley Camp story was by no means over. It became the home of German prisoners of war awaiting repatriation and was used by a succession of British Army units.The memories linger. For thousands of Brits and Americans the whispering grass of Wolverley still tells its tales. During his research Mike made contact with a retired nurse from the Fightin' 52nd, Barbara Harris. She came over from New York to walk the English fields where she and her colleagues did their life-saving work. 'And she felt exactly the same as us,' smiles Mike Webster. 'She said she felt a presence. It's as though the hospital is still there.'
June 2008

Death of a Lancaster
Never approach a wounded beast. The Lancaster bomber was one of the most ferocious beasts of the Second World War. Even in its death throes it could kill. It was the night of 24 February 1944. Sergeant Jim Chapman was on his thirtieth bombing mission, 20,000 feet above the German city of Schweinfurt. The target, a ball-bearing factory. He was a twenty-three-year-old veteran of raids on Berlin, Hamburg and the Nazi secret-weapon site at Peenemunde, the rear gunner in the Lancaster, the most dangerous job in Bomber Command. 'At one stage the statisticians told us a rear gunner's life expectancy was fifteen minutes,' he recalls at his home in Willenhall. But it suited him. Earlier he had served as the upper gunner, with a panoramic view as the Lancaster fleets headed towards the deadly hosepipes of tracer fire and flashes of anti-aircraft shells. These were scenes from hell. Five miles below a German city was consumed by a firestorm. Up in the heavens a swarm of cannon shells

sought out the RAF bombers. 'I could see too much and I thought it was going to affect my mind. I'd rather sit at the back and see where we had been – not where we were going.'After the Schweinfurt raid he could look forward to six months out of combat as an instructor. But on the final approach to the factory, his luck ran out. 'Suddenly there was this noise surrounding my turret, like rattling a stick along corrugated iron. Then I was aware of this glow beneath me.'Unknown to him, a German night fighter had ripped the centre of the Lancaster apart with cannon fire. The 4,000 pound bomb load was smoking and the plane was doomed. The pilot's voice crackled over the intercom: 'Bale out!'Easier said than done. The rear gunner sat in an exposed steel-frame turret. His parachute was stowed behind him. 'Suddenly it really dawned on me that I was at war. It took an eternity to get out.'So long, in fact, that the German pilot returned to the stricken Lancaster, now blazing from end to end. How could he have known that Jim Chapman and the upper gunner were still in their turrets, each armed with four machine-guns? For the first and last time in the Second World War Sergeant Chapman fired in anger. 'He was no more than 5 feet above us. We didn't have time to aim but we didn't need to. It was pure reaction. We couldn't miss him. I got a good burst off and down he went. I remember thinking the one word – bastard.'With hindsight, he smiles; that German pilot probably saved his life. Jim Chapman baled out safely and spent the rest of the war in POW camps. In 1939–45 RAF Bomber Command lost 55,888 aircrew killed, of whom 28,350 were air gunners. Ten thousand more were shot down and captured. Ironically, the most terrifying moment of Sergeant Chapman's war came just a few days before liberation in May 1945 when he was part of a column of prisoners of war shot up by RAF Typhoons. But soon he was safe home with his wife Vera, who had endured six months of agony, not knowing whether he was dead or alive.But for Bomber Command there was little post-war recognition and no campaign medal. Even before the war was over the mass slaughter in German cities caused by Allied bombing was troubling some consciences. Jim Chapman describes the sight of blazing German cities as 'awesome' and admits he felt occasional twinges of remorse, 'but you just got on with it'.Before the war Jim served as a Territorial with the South Staffordshire Regiment. He volunteered for the RAF. He takes great pride in having helped to smash the Nazi war machine, especially by hitting Berlin and the V1 and V2 works at Peenemunde. 'But I'd have had more recognition and appreciation if I'd stayed in the regiment. No-one ever said thank you to us. I feel hard done to.' *November 2004*

Background to D-Day

Three nightmares haunted the top brass as the greatest invasion fleet in history sailed for Normandy: Dunkirk – the retreat from France by the

British Expeditionary Force in 1940; Dieppe – the ill-conceived raid on the French port in 1942, which left thousands of British and Canadian troops dead, wounded or captured; and Slapton Sands: weeks before D-Day an American force had been surprised and torn apart by German E-boats while on exercise with landing craft off the Devon coast. No-one needed reminding about Dunkirk. Although the propagandists had enjoyed a field day with fine talk about miracles and deliverance, many of the old sweats who sailed for Normandy on 5 June knew better. They had seen Allied resistance fall apart under the German blitzkrieg of 1940. They had seen the French throw in the towel with barely a fight. They had seen second-rate British tanks shot to pieces by superior German ones. They had cowered for days in the ditches and beaches around Dunkirk, picked off by Stuka dive-bombers and wondering what had happened to the RAF. And later they had heard horror stories of slow, under-armed RAF fighter-bombers being swatted effortlessly out of the skies by the Luftwaffe. In Normandy they were promised total air superiority. And although the Germans still had the technological edge in heavy tanks and were supremely skilled with mortars, the Allies had overwhelming power.

But the lads had been told similar gung-ho stuff before the raid on Dieppe. Lord Louis Mountbatten later claimed that D-Day was won on the beaches of Dieppe in August 1942. Others saw the so-called 'reconnaissance in strength' as a costly fiasco, mounted solely to boost morale in Russia and convince Stalin that the West was serious about opening a second front against Hitler. The Dieppe Raid involved a Canadian division and three British Commando regiments. More than 3,500, half of those taking part, were killed, wounded or captured. The slaughter of unprotected Canadian infantry on the beaches was pitiful. Of 4,963 Canadians who sailed from Southampton, only 2,210 returned the next day.'They were a grand bunch of blokes,' recalls Dieppe Raid veteran George Jones, of Wednesfield. We knew it was just a raid but I think some of the Canadians thought they were in Dieppe to stay'. His unit, 4 Commando, knocked out some German heavy guns but escaped by the skin of its teeth. He had to swim the last quarter-mile from the beach to a landing craft.

John Whorton of Lilleshall, Shropshire, an eighteen-year-old commanding a Churchill tank at Dieppe, watched in horror as his tank, never tested in shingle, sank deep into the beach. 'The tracks just went round and round and the German guns had not been knocked out. We were sitting targets.' Wounded twice, he and a comrade escaped. The other three crewmen were killed.

Dieppe taught the Allies two lessons: it was impossible to seize a French port intact; and infantry landing without tanks were sitting ducks. That is why, for D-Day, the Allies took their own port with them in the shape of the prefabricated Mulberry harbours whose massive caissons can still be seen on the French beaches. They took tanks, too, everything from conventional Sherman tanks to a vast range of 'Funnies', designed to destroy minefields, demolish pillboxes, cross deep trenches and squirt blazing jets of fire.

For the Americans, the awful memory of Slapton Sands was too fresh to forget. So they kept it quiet. At the end of April a full-scale rehearsal for Utah and Omaha beaches had been staged on the shingle beach at Devon, but as a convoy of nine US landing craft sailed through Lyme Bay heading for Slapton they were attacked by nine German E-boats. Many perished in the shell fire, others burned to death and some took their chances in the water and drowned. Bodies of young Americans were washed up for days afterwards. In all, 749 died. Local people were told to say nothing; even American commanders were kept in the dark about the full scale of the tragedy: the American General Omar Bradley was told, and believed until four years after the war, that Slapton was 'a minor brush with the enemy'. In fact it was one of the major tragedies of the European war, and risked exposing the entire Allied plan. Fourteen of the missing Americans were special forces officers who knew the precise location of the landing beaches in Normandy. Were they captured? Had they been interrogated by the Nazis and given their secrets away?

For a fortnight the Allied top brass agonised. Then the last of the bodies was washed up on the Dorset coast. The secret was intact. D-Day was on. *May 1994*

Operation Jericho

D-Day could not have succeeded without total secrecy and the support of the French Resistance. As the time for the invasion drew near, Allied top brass faced a double dilemma. Hundreds of French freedom fighters and a number of British secret agents were held in the Nazi jail in the French city of Amiens. Some already had detailed information about D-Day; some were due to be executed by firing squad. At the request of the French Resistance the RAF prepared Operation Jericho, a daring plan to smash the prison open and set the prisoners free. Three squadrons of high-speed Mosquito bombers were given the job. Flight Sergeant George King, a twenty-four-year-old from Tipton, was at the heart of the mission. At Hunsdon airfield near London he was a fitter/armourer responsible for setting the fuses on the bombs. He recalls every detail: 'Each 500lb bomb had an eleven-second delay to give the aircraft time to get clear. It was absolutely on-the-deck flying at 50 feet.' The weather on 18 February 1944 was atrocious, but the prisoner executions were imminent and the Mosquitoes went off to war, skimming the sea on the brief cross-Channel hop to Amiens. Operation

Jericho was short, bloody and successful. As with the biblical tale of Jericho, the walls came a-tumbling down. The bombs primed by George King and his team smashed the perimeter and the prison buildings, releasing 258 of the 700 prisoners. Sadly, a further 102 were killed by the bombing.Two Mosquitoes were shot down during the attack, including the one flown by Group Captain Charles Pickard. He and his navigator, Flight Lieutenant Alan Broadley, were killed. An hour after the raid the ground crew counted the bombers back and realised Pickard, their Commanding Officer, was missing. 'He was a very good CO. I remember when he set up the wing he set a deadline and said if we were operational in time he'd throw a party. And what a party it was – he had thirty-six barrels of beer lined up along the side of one hangar.'As the RAF crews mourned their CO, the escaped Resistance fighters in France set about planning for D-Day. On the night of the invasion, 5–6 June 1944, thousands of acts of sabotage took place across Normandy, wrecking German communications and spreading confusion as the Allies slipped ashore. George King's squadron was soon operating from a captured Luftwaffe airfield in France, where his own courage was put to the test. When fire broke out in an old German bomb dump he was part of the team that fought desperately to put out the blaze, saving both airfield and nearby village from devastation. George was mentioned in dispatches. 'It was self-preservation. Either we put it out, or it put us out.' *May 2004*

The Longest Day
It was mid-August 1944 and Edith Jones, a seventeen-year-old munitions worker, was walking home for lunch when a distraught neighbour rushed up. 'Have you heard the terrible news about Tom?'The words still haunt her. She raced home to find the family in tears. The dreaded telegram had arrived. Her brother Tom, just nineteen and the pride of the street, had been killed in the fierce fighting at the river Orne in Normandy. He was one of about 37,000 Allied troops who never came home. No-one in the family made the pilgrimage over the Channel to visit Tom Jones's grave, until this day in 1994, when, overwhelmed by tears and drenched by a sudden spring shower from a leaden Normandy sky, his sister, now Edith Wythe, of Wednesfield, paid her respects. Private 14420218 Thomas Jones lies in plot 22 of Bayeux war cemetery, row C, grave 12, alongside five comrades of the South Staffordshire Regiment.'He was a lovely man, lovely,' Edith recalls, wiping her eyes as she lays a posy for remembrance on the immaculately tended grave. 'He wanted to join up as soon as the war started. They took him when he was seventeen-and-a-half and we only saw him twice on leave. The second leave was supposed to be for fourteen days, but after five days he was called back for D-Day. We never saw him again.'A few hours later this coachful of veterans and well-wishers reaches the invasion beaches, where every

house and café seems to be decked with red, white and blue banners: 'Welcome to Our Liberators'. Reuben Welsh of Brewood, a tank radio operator who fought on D-Day with the Staffordshire Yeomanry, holds the coach spellbound. 'See, here?' He points out where his Sherman tanks roared ashore 'without even getting our tracks wet' and raced inland to grab the high ground on 6 June 1944. It was a shrewd move. As German tanks launched a counter-attack the Staffordshire Yeomanry shot them to pieces.'They didn't come back again,' he says grimly.

And big, brave George Jones of Wednesfield, who got stuck into some of the bloodiest fighting with his pals in the Commandos, has so much to say but is choked by emotion. This is his first trip back in fifty years, and as we catch sight of Pegasus Bridge the 6-foot figure in the green beret breaks down. Between the beach and this bridge, 4 miles inland, George's five hundred Commandos were shot and shelled to shreds. All but eighty were killed or wounded. 'I'm full up. I'm very emotional. If you weren't there, you can't imagine it,' he says, handing over the microphone at the front of the coach.'You're entitled to be emotional, mate,' someone whispers.

Alf 'Tug' Wilson, aged seventy-four, of Bloxwich, is offered the mike, but no thanks, he insists, he can't follow a tale like that. Maybe tomorrow, but not just now. Anyway, he didn't do much, really. What he actually did on D-Day, for the record, was fly an unarmed, engineless Horsa glider into a Normandy bristling with enemy guns. Oh, and as he was landing, another Horsa crashed on top of him with 'one hell of a bang', but he got down safely. That was all. The things these impossibly brave young men did all those years ago bring tears to the toughest eyes. Old soldiers never talk about killing people, simply of 'doing the job or 'doing what we were told', a neat shorthand which removes them from the terrors that still cause sleepless nights. For years afterwards, says Reuben Welsh, he couldn't enjoy a drive in the countryside without seeing every wood as a tank hiding place, every valley as an ambush. George Jones remembers a German officer decapitated by a shell, his hat nearby, his head nowhere to be seen 'and not a drop of blood anywhere'.

And yet it is impossible to be here in Normandy at this time, amid this incredible sea of goodwill and mounting excitement, where people spot a British number plate and smile and wave, and to stay maudlin for long. The gratitude of the Normans is both humbling and extraordinary. Seventeen thousand French civilians perished in the D-Day operation and its aftermath. Every town was bombed and blasted to rubble. Reuben Welsh remembers each Sherman in his regiment pumping fifty shells a day into the German-held hamlet of La Bijude. Today it sports a plaque, proudly declaring itself 'the most destroyed village in Normandy'. At Pegasus Bridge, stormed by British glider troops in the opening minutes of D-Day, a bevy of thirtysomething French women cyclists flirt with the old English warriors. 'You were here?' they ask the former tank crewman. 'Impossible. You're too young. Such a young face, non?' Eighty-year-old Madame Marie Guiffard pushes her way forward through the laughing throng. Monsieur Welsh was at Hermanville on D-Day? Why, that was her village. She was thirty, expecting a baby, and her family lived in a slit trench in the garden for five weeks during 'le debarquement', the invasion. She remembers the commandos coming up the road led by a bagpiper. Was that Reuben, peut-être? 'Non, pas moi,' he explains in the French he has learned at night school since he was seventy. 'J'etais dans un char.' 'Ah, oui, les chars!' she exclaims. She remembers the tanks. And she remembers the first night of 6 June when a young, exhausted English soldier flopped into the slit trench and fell fast asleep. But, alors, such a sleep. The Tommy was shaking with spasms and the family was so terrified that they took his rifle away in case he suddenly woke and started shooting. She summons a little English: 'Thank you, thank you for everything.' And a handshake turns into one, two, three kisses on the cheek in the Norman fashion. Her husband comes forward to shake the old soldiers' hands, any hands, English hands.

That night, over dinner, the conversation darkens, as it tends to when old folk gather. What was it all for? Look at the state of the country now. Kids today, have you seen them? Useless. No respect. 'Actually, now I think of it,' says Reuben Welsh, the twinkle still in his eye from Pegasus Bridge, 'my father used to say my generation was rubbish, too. But we didn't do too badly, did we?' *May 1994*

Air assault

The invasion plan was simple. Allied troops would land on five beaches and grab a slice of Normandy 50 miles wide. British and American airborne troops would strike a few miles inland to seal off the left and right flanks of the invasion area. From this bridgehead the liberation of Europe would begin. The first victory of D-Day fell to the men of the British 6th Airborne Division. Their job was to secure two crucial bridges and protect the eastern flank of the invasion area from German reinforcements. Out of a squally sky six huge gliders carrying 180 men of the Oxford & Buckinghamshire Light Infantry slewed to a standstill within yards of the bridges. Albert Gregory of Stourbridge, a twenty-nine -year-old medic, was on the third glider to touch down at the Caen Canal bridge (later renamed Pegasus Bridge in honour of the Airborne Division badge) just after midnight on 6 June. The six-glider assault was led by Major John Howard. Pegasus Bridge was seized in less than ten minutes in a flurry of grenades and machine-gun fire. The nearby Orne bridge fell with barely a shot being fired. 'I didn't know what to expect. I'd never been in action before and every time I got in the glider I was always sick because of the smell of glue and stale vomit. It was awful. But on D-Day itself I wasn't sick. Maybe that's because I was scared stiff. We had a bit of a bumpy landing. One wing broke off on a post and we spun round like a top. I looked after one man in our glider who had a broken leg. The next glider was smashed up and one of the spars had splintered and gone through a chap's back. He was dead.' As Albert Gregory and his comrades held Pegasus Bridge against German counter-attacks, Frank Swann of Coseley was one of hundreds of paras dropped all over Normandy and converging on the bridge as reinforcements. At 11.30pm he and the rest of HQ company of 5 Parachute Brigade climbed aboard their aircraft. Like Albert, he enjoyed his first sickness-free flight. 'As we got near the French coast the order came to hook up. Then all hell broke loose. The enemy anti-aircraft fire was very good and the plane took evasive action. We all ended up on the floor. We just managed to get up when the hatch was opened and out we went. The sky was alight with flares and ack-ack fire.' Landing safely, he bumped into his brigade commander, Brigadier Nigel Poett and escorted him through the battle. 'I had to laugh. He was 6 foot 6 inches with only his side arms and a map. I was 5 foot 4 inches carrying 100 lbs of equipment. Talk about the long and the short. We were the first paratroops to reach Pegasus Bridge. What a night.' Alec Harper of Bloxwich, a staff-sergeant in the Paras, dropped into Normandy through 'a firework display' of tracer bullets and made his way to Pegasus Bridge. His war began at 10.15pm on 5 June as he and his comrades boarded the Stirling bombers that were to drop them over Normandy. In the dim fuselage, he recalled, there was little for the paras to do but chat to the next man and contemplate the chances of survival: 'Will I end up at the Hippodrome with a couple of pints of Butler's or Banks's . . . ?' Over the French coast tracer shells flashed past the Stirlings. The red light came on and the paras prepared to go. As the green light showed they jumped into the blackness, falling towards occupied France. 'Jerry was firing everything at hand. Searchlights were sweeping the sky and tracer bullets seemed to be coming from everywhere. It was like a fireworks display but instead of looking at it, one was in the middle of it.' His abiding memory of D-Day was the unearthly wail of bagpipes echoing over the meadows when Lord Lovat's Commandos arrived as reinforcements, having fought their way inland from the invasion beaches. Bold as brass, Piper Bill Millin was making his way up the road at the head of the Commando Brigade. Lovat's men had stormed ashore on the beaches at dawn and fought their way inland, relieving small pockets of determined but lightly armed paras and gliderborne troops who had been in action all night.

Advance parties of two para brigades landed at twenty minutes after midnight on 6 June. Lieutenant Stan Jeavons of Bilston, serving with the Parachute Regiment's 13th Battalion, was among them. He made an 'uneventful' landing beside a railway line and rallied his platoon near the village of Ranville. As they gathered in the darkness an uncomfortable truth dawned. He smiles as he remembers clearly his first words to his lads: 'Look around. There's no other buggers here but us.' He says: 'It was terribly exciting to realise, deep down, that we were on our bloody own. We were so isolated I seriously thought the invasion had been cancelled.' Years later a senior officer told him that he and his little band of brothers were dropped as a diversion, designed to draw German forces away from the main glider and parachute landing zones. If so, they succeeded. From the moment they hit the ground the 13th Battalion were under fire. Through the next day they fought off three ferocious German attacks on Ranville. And as the Germans threw guns and tanks against the invasion, the lightly armed Paras fought almost to exhaustion.

Later in the campaign Stan Jeavons faced a bizarre duel. From the enemy lines 200 yards away a German officer rose, waving a rifle, bayonet glistening in the Normandy sun. As a band of British paras watched fascinated, the solitary German advanced. Someone pushed a Lee-Enfield rifle into the hands of the twenty-six-year-old lieutenant. Stan Jeavons climbed out of the trench and awaited the foe. But if the Nazi wanted some bizarre, noble duel, Lieutenant Jeavons certainly did not. 'This bloke seemed to be thinking of a bayonet fight. It was the last thing I had in mind. When he got within a few yards I shot him dead.' Stan Jeavons's luck ran out a few weeks after D-Day. As enemy shells rained down his batman, Private Prew, was having a quick smoke in the bottom of the trench. 'The shelling was terrible and then suddenly – slap! – one landed straight on the trench. I was buried. They managed to dig out my head but the shelling was so bad they had to leave me.' For the next few minutes he endured the hellish experience of being buried neck-deep in Normandy, bullets cracking around his exposed head, unable to move a limb or even draw his revolver. His batman was buried alive and suffocated. Losing blood from leg wounds, Lieutenant Jeavons slipped into a coma and awoke days later in a military hospital in Britain. His army days were over.

Para John Lunt of Aldridge dropped at about 1am but landed 5 miles off target in the middle of an entire brigade's drop zone: 'There were two thousand people coming down, containers and steel helmets going everywhere. It was bloody dangerous. Confusion was the order of the night.' High over occupied France in a converted Halifax bomber crammed with paras, twenty-year-old Fred Browning of Alveley near Bridgnorth heard a strange new sound. It was the sound of German bullets hitting the Halifax. Fred and his pals knew it was time to get out. They parachuted into Normandy in the opening minutes of D-Day. His unit, the 700 men of the Parachute Regiment's 12th battalion, was widely scattered but he joined a small group and set off into battle. 'We were straight into one or two skirmishes. It was bloody exciting. We all enjoyed it.'The battalion's job on D-Day was to reinforce Major John Howard's little force, which had seized two vital bridges. The lightly armed paras were to hold the bridges until they were relieved. It was hard, bloody work. But the worst was to come six days later when the Germans, supported by tanks, launched two attacks on the paras. As they withdrew over a bridge the Brits came under sniper fire. Fred vividly recalls how a Commando sergeant grabbed the body of a dead German, put a red beret on its head and pushed the corpse over the parapet. The trick worked. The sniper fired, revealing his hiding place, and was instantly killed. 'He was a German soldier but he only looked fourteen or fifteen.'Walter Johnson of Stourbridge was part of the Parachute Regiment's Ninth Battalion (9 Para), whose job on D-Day was to smash the Merville Battery, a maze of minefields, bunkers and barbed wire containing four big guns aimed at the invasion beaches. Seven hundred paras trained for the attack. But on the night of 5 June they flew into heavy German fire. The battalion was scattered all over the coastal area and lost all its heavy weapons. Only 150 paras showed up for the assault, less than a quarter of the force. Even so, they attacked and destroyed the Merville Battery, killing two hundred German defenders. About fifty paras died in the attack.

They had taken off from a Cotswold airfield just as night fell on 5 June. Walter recalls the runway lined with WAAFs, girls from the Women's Auxiliary Air Force, 'and they were all crying'. As they reached the French coast the sky filled with German tracer bullets. 'I could see flak coming through the fuselage. We got the order "stand up!" and I realised the plane was diving, which was not right. I jumped, and I can still see the guns blazing away at us. Then this water was coming up to me in the moonlight.'Walter was terrified of landing in the sea. Instead, he crashed into a tree and was stuck for twenty minutes before he could cut himself free. 'I skinned my hands and I'd lost my kit. I had no rifle, nothing but my knife and two grenades. I didn't see another soul for over an hour.'In ones and twos, through a squally night with clouds blowing across the moon, the paras made their way to Merville. When he had about a hundred and fifty men, the Commanding Officer, Lieutenant -Colonel Terence Otway, decided to attack. 'The noise was terrific,' says Wally Johnson. 'The Germans had sixteen machine-guns on us. Something hit me in the hand. Then someone threw a phosphorous grenade and I went straight into it. There was smoke and dead bodies everywhere.' It was all over in less than fifteen minutes. Shocked, drenched in blood from shrapnel wounds and with a bullet hole clean through his right hand, he crawled out of the battery with five German prisoners. As the battered, bleeding paras wrecked the German guns and withdrew, the scale of their losses became clear. 'There were only sixty-five of us came out and only about thirty of them were any use,' says the old soldier, whose wounds put him out of action for months. Harry Pagett of Heath Town, Wolverhampton, was one of many of Wally Johnson's comrades in 9 Para who went wildly off course on the night of 5–6 June. D-Day was his first, and last, taste of action. 'Twenty of us were dropped into occupied territory to knock out the coastal guns. But something went wrong. We landed 20 miles away from where we should have been. We tried to walk it, but kept running into the Germans. When we had lost twelve men and ran out of ammunition our sergeant said it was suicide to go on. So we surrendered.' Harry Pagett spent the rest of the war in POW camps. James Rose from Darlaston was one of the paras killed in action at the Merville Battery. His body was found near the battery three days after the epic attack. His nephew, Jim Wheeler, later donated memorabilia to the world-famous Pegasus Bridge museum, including the telegram of condolence from the Queen to James's mother, photographs and letters from his commanding officer.John Denis Potts from Cannock was a glider pilot whose D-Day ended in captivity. His aircraft, with twenty-four soldiers on board, left the English mainland at about 10pm on 5 June. He flew straight into a massive 600-strong Lancaster attack at Le Havre. Amid the bombardment his glider was shot down at about 1am. Everyone survived the crash-landing, almost on top of a German Army HQ. 'I was out first and almost immediately we could hear the Germans coming. They probably thought they had shot a bomber down, so they were surprised when they saw us and the glider.' Wounded in the crossfire, he was forced to face the German media, paraded as a prisoner of war. It was exactly a year before he returned home. Sergeant Kurt Fromm, of Bentley, dropped into Normandy early on D-Day as part of the oddest military unit in the British Army. Born in Ireland of a German father, he joined Number 3 Troop of 10 Commando, an elite unit made up entirely of German speakers and jokingly dubbed the King's Own Enemy Aliens. A liaison officer between the airborne and seaborne forces, he would not have lasted long if he had fallen into German hands. So he had a false identity: 'Sergeant McGregor'. He was also one of the few D-Day warriors with his name already on a war memorial in France. A veteran of the Spanish Civil War, Kurt Fromm had joined the French Foreign Legion and was 'missing, presumed dead' on the retreat to Dunkirk in 1940.Alf Garratt of Wollaston, Stourbridge, was a twenty-two-year-old driver-mechanic, part of a six-man unit in a glider with an anti-tank gun and a jeep. Their aircraft crash-landed in a field after being hit by flak, which also hit the underside of their jeep as they sat on top of it. 'The landing wasn't too bad. It could have been worse. It was a bit hairy when we came down in all the flak; it wasn't pleasant.'The team headed towards the village of Ranville, where they set the gun up in an orchard. 'It sloped down to a cornfield and the idea was to put the gun in the hedge facing the cornfield in case anything came across it. They came into our sights and we had the advantage of seeing them first, so that was the end of three German tanks.'Frank Payne of Cradley Heath, a machine-gunner in the Parachute Regiment, landed safely and set up his gun but had to leave it behind in the rush to rejoin his battalion. 'I noticed a tank with an 88mm gun and, as I warned the lads, it fired, killing one lad and wounding all the others except me. I managed to drag and walk some of the section back to Ranville, all with shrapnel wounds.' The afternoon was spent guarding the landing grounds from counter-attack. He recalled how the gliders came in 'like cars in a car park, some failing to get in and smashing through brick walls.'

Naval bombardment

At 5.30 am on 6 June, as the paras and glider troops held their hard-won positions inland, thousands of British and American naval guns opened fire on the beaches. No-one who witnessed that earth-shattering bombardment will ever forget it. Some of the battleships were firing 16-inch shells almost as long as a car and so big that they could clearly been seen, and felt, as they went past. Inland, as one massive shell roared over, Major John Howard's signaller turned to his officer and said, 'Blimey, sir, they're firing Jeeps.'Bill Sharples of Pattingham was a nineteen-year-old signaller on the minesweeper HMS *Llandudno*. The ship was 'almost blown out of the water' when the nearby HMS *Ramilies* and *Ajax* opened fire. Later he and his shipmates had the grim task of recovering identity tags from the floating bodies of soldiers killed in the attack. Harry Anderson of Chapel Ash, Wolverhampton, was a lance-corporal and fitter, aged twenty-four, with the 4th/7th Dragoon Guards. He recalls the incredible concussion of the bombardment. 'We were by HMS *Warspite* and every salvo she fired lifted our landing craft up, almost out of the water.'Jack Hill, of Quarry Bank, was a stoker-mechanic on a minesweeper off Gold Beach. Dawn broke as they approached the French coast: 'A landing craft, just astern and starboard, hit a mine. Black smoke poured from it but, as orders forbade us to stop, we carried on. The Royal Navy ships began the bombardment of installations ashore. Battleships, destroyers, cruisers and even monitors from the First World War with their huge guns all took part. The noise of the guns firing and the shells whizzing overhead was terrifying.'

Able Seaman John Fletcher of Sedgley, was just eighteen and a 'tankie' in charge of rations on the destroyer HMS *Talybont*. The warship supported the epic US Rangers' attack on German gun batteries at Point du Hoc. 'I was a loader on the stern 4-inch gun. It was not a closed turret but an open position with an armour shield. The shells weighed 56 pounds each, and in those days I could carry one in each arm. Our targets on D-Day were machine-gun nests and a radar station on the coast. A couple of big cruisers were behind us. When they opened up you could feel the heat of their shells going overhead.'

Later, *Talybont* had a deadlier job. 'We were bait. Our job was to draw the fire of big German guns near Le Havre. They were only firing at night to avoid giving away their position. We sailed up and down but they didn't fire. So the captain gave the order to 'splice the mainbrace' and line the men up on the upper deck for the daily rum ration. They lined up and I served it out. The idea was to show the Germans we weren't in the least concerned about them. Well, that got them firing, but their shells were falling short of us. We reported their positions and that night the RAF blew them off their site.'

Three miles off the Normandy coast, David Phillips of Merry Hill, Wolverhampton, was a young Royal Marines NCO with a grandstand view of the invasion as dawn broke on D-Day: 'Our ship was in the van of a vast armada of ships which stretched from horizon to horizon. It was a thrilling and awesome spectacle and I felt a glow of pride and patriotism in the knowledge that I was taking part in this historic enterprise which would be remembered long after I was dead. On the morning of D-Day we were firing broadsides and the whole ship rocked. It seemed the sea was full of vessels. You couldn't see anything for ships. I remember feeling a bit querulous, but we had the feeling that everything was going to plan because we had air superiority.'*Scylla* closed on the shore and her mighty broadsides silenced the German guns one by one. Later, transferred into a landing craft, David Phillips and his comrades headed for Juno beach: 'The first wave of British and Canadians had already breached the first line of enemy defences, leaving behind scores of dead bodies, some of which floated in the surf while others covered the shoreline. I shall never forget the peculiarly sweet smell of death which pervaded the area.'He had joined the Royal Navy at his father Bill's request, in the hope of being spared such carnage. Bill had been wounded at the bloody battle of Passchendaele in the First World War. David recalls the 'sudden 300-mile dash' into Belgium and Holland after the Normandy campaign, and his own appointment with destiny. 'It was towards the end of 1944 in Antwerp. German flying bombs were landing at the rate of one every two minutes. You could almost set your watch by them. One of them hit a cinema full of civilians and there were about 500 casualties. We got the injured out and rescued some others.'He talks quietly, modestly, about this act of courage and humanity that won him the Belgian gallantry decoration, the Croix de Guerre.

Beach landings

Long before the Allied armada hit the Normandy beaches, midget submarines were only a few yards offshore, watching from the shallows. Some 'sneaky-beaky' units were silently creeping ashore. Jack Palmer from Netherton was one of the first. His tiny Royal Signals detachment was landed at dead of night to provide radio systems for the invading army: 'By 3.30am on 6 June we pulled into shallow water on the Normandy coast. We disembarked in a hurry. The skipper seemed rather anxious to be away. Pulling the cable carrier up the beach proved to be a hell of a job. In the dark a number of steel tripods had to be circumvented. Unknown to us they were heavily mined. Fortunately there were no mishaps. It was quiet as the grave with not a soul anywhere, least of all German troops. We led the invasion on D-Day!'

Stan Twyman of Codsall was a mere boy, an eighteen-year-old midshipman on an armoured tank-landing craft, LCT (A) 2238. In the grey, squally morning of D-Day he gave the most momentous order of his life. On the approach to Gold Beach some landing craft struck submerged mines and blew up. Others were holed and vanished in seconds. But his made a text-book run-in to the beach. 'Ramp down!' shouted the teenager, securing his place in history. The steel ramp fell forward. His cargo, a flail tank designed to carve paths through minefields, moved steadily down the ramp. The landing craft next to his was stranded on the beach, unable to withdraw. Another landing craft nearby was shattered by an enemy shell. 'We were lucky. It was a very quiet section of the beach. But none of these landings ever went as planned. You just went in. All I can recall is this feeling that we were doing our job. I suddenly realised on the way across the Channel that this was a very, very big thing. There was this huge armada – and most of it seemed to be behind us.' The ramps went down and the lads of the Dorset Regiment stormed ashore. They were in the first wave of the D-Day landings on Gold Beach.

'You can't begin to describe it,' recalls Norman Horton of Great Wyrley. 'Everything was blowing up. There was shrapnel and bodies everywhere. All you think about is yourself. All you can do is get across the beach and into cover as fast as possible.'

The race over the sands took a matter of minutes. As part of the 50th Division, the Dorsets were chosen to lead the attack on Hitler's much-vaunted Atlantic Wall. At first tanks could not be used. It was a classic infantry battle of sudden death and shredded nerves. 'There were snipers everywhere. You never knew where the enemy was. You'd be talking to a pal one day and the next day he'd be gone. There were different faces all the times as new men arrived to fill the gaps.'By the end of 6 June 1944 the twenty-four-year-old private was dug in with his company at a village inland from Arromanches. 'We took that village and lost it six times. 'It was never a pushover.'Jim Drew from Tipton was a twenty-year-old sergeant, also with the Dorset Regiment. 'The ramp went down and we stepped out, right up to our chests in water. Some of our comrades just went straight under because of the equipment they were wearing. The sea was red with blood.'

Pinned down by fire, his unit was saved by one of the 'Funnies', a flail tank that smashed its way through a minefield. 'Our orders were to get as far inland as we could to secure a bridgehead. We advanced faster than anyone thought. We were about three miles inland when suddenly shells from our own guns started dropping all around us. My company commander had his arm blown off and I was blown up with shrapnel all over me.' Jim was not expected to survive, and spent a year in a military hospital. Horace Hill from Cradley trained for months on one of the top-secret weapons that helped win D-Day. The story began with a tragedy. Two years before D-Day the Allies' raid on Dieppe ended in disaster. Clearly, infantry on a beach were sitting ducks. So a few months later Major-General Percy Hobart was brought out of retirement to devise a range of armoured vehicles to make the beaches safe. The result was 'Hobart's Funnies', a bizarre assortment of converted tanks designed to blow up pillboxes, cross gaps, lay bridges, detonate minefields and squirt flame. Horace recalls the 'Funnies' with pride. As a sergeant in the 79th Armoured Division, he commanded a Churchill tank fitted with a vast 'bobbin' of steel-reinforced track. As the tank advanced the bobbin unwound, and the track turned treacherous clay and sand into a road fit for armies. 'We had been trained to go over, under or through any obstacle in our way. And that included demolishing anything up to 14 feet of concrete.'He was in the first wave, at 7.30am on D-Day. As the landing craft crunched on to the beach a shell tore into the next craft, killing an officer. Mr Hill recalls 'a few bodies lying around'. But by the fortunes of war, he had been dropped in a quiet sector of the beach. His 'Funny' went forward into 6 feet of water and made straight for its allotted task. The only snag was a jammed bobbin. It was heaved into place by a group of soldiers and one war reporter. Sergeant Cox erected a green windsock to mark Exit No. 4, Mike Green Sector, Juno Beach. Job done. Hitler's troops, using slave labour, had spent four years building the defences known as the Atlantic Wall to keep the Allies out. Horace Hill and thousands of his pals punched a hole through it in about half an hour.Bill Hawkins, a blacksmith from Rawnsley in peacetime, was the demolition expert on a Churchill tank 'Funny' put ashore on Juno Beach to destroy German gun positions. But as the tank struggled ashore, it sank in a flooded culvert. He and his Royal Engineers crew all survived and scrambled out. On the beach they huddled together for shelter, but a German mortar bomb found them. Four of the six were killed. Bill suffered an arm wound and lost his left eye and part of his cheek. For him, the war was over. For years he never told his wife, Joan, what had happened to him on D-Day. All was revealed in 1976 when the French authorities at Graye-sur-Mer recovered the rusting Churchill tank and mounted it on a plinth where it proudly overlooks the invasion beach. Bill was one of the guests-of-honour at the unveiling of the monument.

The day before D-Day twenty-year-old Charles Scott from Quarry Bank and his comrades in the East Riding Yeomanry were told they had a mere 25 per cent chance of surviving the next forty-eight hours. They were in the first wave to assault Sword Beach in amphibious tanks. 'The Navy were very good. We were dropped right on the beaches by the landing craft. To be honest, some of the lads were happy to be on the ground again because they had become sea sick. I don't think they quite understood what a horrific situation we were being dropped into. There was just so much action going on, planes and gliders all over the skies, some being shot down, somersaulting in the air before crashing into the ground or into the tanks.'

A German 88mm gun shot down one of the British gliders. Retribution from the Yeomanry was swift and deadly. 'Immediately nearly all of the squadron turned towards him and shot at him. There was no time to think about what you were doing. The only time you weren't afraid was when you were shooting, carrying out your orders. I saw so much bravery that day. The infantry and the airborne were so courageous.' The Commandos were among the first ashore, scorning steel helmets for their famous green berets. They were led by Lord Lovat and a piper. 'Give us "Highland Laddie", man!' ordered the officer as the commandos hit the beach. Among them was George Jones of Wednesfield who became entangled in some of the bloodiest fighting of the day. Between the beach at Ouistreham and Pegasus Bridge, 4 miles inland, his five hundred-strong unit, No. 4 Commando, was constantly under fire. In the fight for Normandy all but eighty were killed or wounded. Sergeant Clive 'Joe' Stringer from Brownhills was a Commando who went ashore at Juno beach, near St Aubin-sur-Mer. It was a scene of horror, with the advance forces pinned down on the beach. Sergeant Stringer was the first of his section into the water, under constant machine-gun fire. At a heavily fortified strongpoint he was ordered to take his section and blow up the massive wall. With stick grenades exploding round them, they positioned explosives at the foot of the battlement. Sergeant Stringer was hit by shrapnel and covered in blood, with multiple wounds. He fought on regardless and for his courage was awarded the Military Medal, pinned on him by General Montgomery six weeks later.

Stan Whitehouse from Netherton was one of the youngest British squaddies to hit the beaches on 6 June 1944, a seventeen-year-old Black Country lad who lied about his age to get in. He recalled the smallness of a private soldier's war: 'Thirty yards that way and maybe thirty yards behind. That's all you can take in, all you dare to look at.'

Ken Leighfield of Wolverhampton went ashore at 7.30am on Gold Beach at the resort of Arromanches. He was a professional soldier aged twenty-four, a corporal in the Durham Light Infantry who had seen action in Sicily and Malta. He is eternally gratefully for having had his baptism of fire before D-Day. 'When you first go into an attack you think you can kill everyone. You find out very quickly that they can kill you, too. The two ramps went down. All I told my section was to get off the beach as quick as they could and not stop for anything. Suddenly I was up to my waist in water. I must have looked like a water rat.'His unit had a successful D-Day. But a few days later Corporal Leighfield was leading a patrol inland towards a farmhouse. 'We cut a big gap in some barbed wire. I called the patrol forward then – bang! – and then shells started exploding.' The first impact was a machine-gun bullet, which bowled him over and left him seriously wounded. On that fateful day his 120-strong company suffered ninety men killed or wounded.Bill Bennett of Kidderminster was an eighteen-year-old able seaman in the Merchant Navy. He went ashore on Gold Beach totally unarmed – yet ended D-Day with an award for gallantry. The teenager was with PLUTO – the remarkable Pipe Line Under The Ocean that pumped petrol from the UK to France to fuel the invasion. He and his colleagues went ashore on Gold Beach, tasked with linking up the pipeline under the sea with the beach. 'The resistance wasn't so bad as we were right under some cliffs, but there were a lot of shells and dive-bombers. I wasn't allowed to carry a gun because I was from the Merchant Navy, although I had to wear a Royal Navy uniform. I didn't really think about having no weapon as I was too busy concentrating on getting the job done. I don't remember any of us talking about being scared. We just got on with it.'

During the morning an engineer with Bill was shot through the shoulder by a fighter plane strafing the beaches and ships. Bill helped transfer the wounded man from the trawler *Grampian* to a destroyer for treatment. This, coupled with his other actions on D-Day, earned him a mention in dispatches.

Ken Parkes of Wednesfield landed on Juno Beach and survived the Normandy Campaign by a miracle. On the push inland his unit was pinned down by German snipers. 'I was with the gun and a shot rang out, with the bullet shattering my rifle. My sergeant-major shouted, "Parkes, get your bloody head down or it'll get shot off." A few minutes later he popped his head up and bang, the sniper got him. He was shot right through the temple.'

Ken Parkes went ashore as a twenty-year-old on a self-propelled anti-tank gun in support of Canadian soldiers leading the assault. 'It was fairly quiet because the bombardment and assault troops were keeping the Germans quiet. The sea was really rough, and the rockets the ships were firing over our heads at the Germans on shore were a fantastic sight. That really made us feel more confident about what we were heading into. Our first attempt to get ashore failed because they tried to drop us too far out for the tanks. We eventually landed in about 3 feet of water, but still managed to get ashore. I remember on the evening of D-Day we thought we had travelled around 10 miles inland. But then an officer came around asking for volunteers to keep going because it turned out we had only gone just over a mile, it just felt more because of all the extra ground we had to cover to avoid gun emplacements and so on. Of course, we all knew you don't volunteer for anything like that, but eventually I think someone else did.'Mr Parkes, from Ashmore Park in Wednesfield, was with the crew of a self-propelled gun mounted on the chassis of a Sherman tank. He stayed with the Canadian troops until they had taken the airfield at Carpiquet in July. 'Then we were used as a roving unit, going where we were needed. We were after the German Panzer tanks. We'd open fire on them from 500 yards. When you hit them with high explosives they just blew right up. But we had to watch out for the German 88mm cannons. If we got caught out by them we were in trouble.'The Americans took the western beaches, codenamed Omaha and Utah. Utah fell miraculously easily, with barely a dozen killed by enemy action and about sixty drowned. But 'Bloody Omaha' was another story. Swept by machine-gun fire and overlooked by gun emplacements on high ground to left and right, Omaha Beach became a 3-mile killing field where more than a thousand Americans perished. Few Brits had any idea what was going on at Omaha. One was Arthur Weston of Oldbury, a twenty-three-year-old radio operator on a wooden motor launch. As he watched thousands of Americans advancing towards the maelstrom he was amazed and horrified: 'My estimation of the Yanks had been pretty low. But seeing them going in, up the beaches, climbing the cliffs, advancing under a hail of machine-gun fire, my opinion changed dramatically. Some of the Americans fell and stayed down, but the green wave of men carried on. I think they should all have had medals as big as dustbin lids.'At one stage the battle-hardened German defenders reported that they had driven the Americans back into the sea at Omaha. Not so. As one US colonel told his boys cowering behind the sea wall, 'The only people on this beach are the dead and those who are going to die. Now let's get the hell out of here!'In countless displays of individual courage young Americans simply got up, crossed the sea wall and moved forward into the gunfire. Sheer guts and relentless shellfire from Allied ships, some coming dangerously close to shore, drove the Germans back.

Sailor Ken Marcham had a grandstand view as the Omaha tragedy unfolded. German guns and mortars tore the American forces apart in scenes later recreated in the movie *Saving Private Ryan*. Watching the nightmare from a mile or more at sea were the Royal Navy ships which had escorted the vast US armada. 'We could only go so far in because of running aground,' recalls Mr Marcham at his home in Bloxwich. 'As the troop carriers went in we could see some of the lads being seasick. It looked as though they dropped their ramps too soon and, with all those heavy packs, the lads didn't stand a chance. A lot of them drowned. It was a shame to see them going in. They were only kids, like us. I thought it was going to be a disaster.'

But as crews in the Allied fleet realised what was happening, they closed on the shore and let fly with every gun on board. 'We blazed away. There were Oerlikon cannons and pom-poms and I'd never seen our four-inch gun so hot. I thought the barrel would melt.'As the navy gunners hammered the German positions the American troops finally blasted their way through the defences and poured inland.Landing-craft Coxswain Len Evans from Wednesbury recalls the bizarre sight of a French torpedo boat playing 'The Marseillaise' at full blast as he piloted his landing craft into the beach and delivered his cargo of troops: 'Some were hit straight away and fell back into the sea. Some were no more than eighteen as I was. One poor lad who had been clearing beach mines floated past us with a perfect hole through his face.'Overloaded with casualties on the return trip, Len Evans's craft sank beneath him. The next thing he recalls he was in a casualty station at Southampton. Photographed by the news-hungry local press, he was hailed the next day as the first Midlander to be wounded in D-Day. Arthur Lloyd of Wednesfield was a tank-landing-craft crewman and a veteran of the Sicily and Italian landings. He recalled seasickness among the soldiers as the craft approached the beaches: 'A sergeant was having trouble with one of his lads. So we gave him a tot of rum – better than the doctor – and I believe he was first up the beach!'

Len Whitehouse of Bilston landed on Gold Beach just after 7am amid a scene of dead and dying. 'It was just after we got on to the beach, I remember seeing my first dead soldier. That really did knock me back.'

The twenty-three-year-old lorry driver with an infantry support unit recalls a fairly straightforward run-in to the beach. 'I'm still grateful to the person who piloted the landing craft. Some of the landing craft didn't make it in close enough and unloaded men and machines too far from the beach. But our chap got through all of the obstructions and everything and got us right to the beach – I didn't even get my wheels wet. I still don't know who he was but I'm grateful to him to this day. We grouped up and moved away from the beach to a field area where we were to unload to establish this airstrip. There was a lot of flak flying around but the first few hours were fairly peaceful for us and our platoon came through all right. There were a few Germans in some woodland near the field but they mainly seemed to be young lads. To be honest I felt a little sorry for them, they looked so down when they were captured. They didn't look like they had much spirit left in them.'David Hall, of Walsall, was a nineteen-year-old Marine piloting a landing craft full of men into Sword Beach early on D-Day. 'We had a real problem getting the boat down into the water from the HMS *Glenearn* because it was a very rough day. At one point it was hanging on the rear hook because the front had been lowered down and the craft, full of soldiers and equipment, was tipping forward. We had to wait for a wave to come up so we could get the back in the water as well. I turned round and saw that the LCT [landing craft] next to ours had caught it. I got to the beach and was told that my cousin, who was on another landing craft, had caught it as well, although I didn't see him, and that really did knock me back. I got the troops and equipment off the boat and was supposed to go back to the ship to collect another load, but it wouldn't go. So I ended up stuck there on the beach. I still get flashbacks and I don't like to recall what I saw there. All I know is that I am here and all my mates are dead and there is no way for me to explain how that feels; what it is like to really hate yourself for being alive.'Getting ashore was seldom as easy as it had been on rehearsal exercises.

Ray Whittingham of Codsall, a twenty-year-old anti-tank gunner, was detailed to help push out a roll of reinforced steel netting from his landing craft to help vehicles drive ashore. Clad in waterproof anti-gas trousers to keep dry, he and his colleagues stepped into chest-high water and their trousers promptly filled with sea water: 'This, together with the inflatable lifebelts that were being worn must have made us appear more like Michelin men than invaders.' Despite their difficulties, they unrolled the matting and the carriers and guns got safely ashore. Stan Cartwright of Cradley Heath was crewman on a landing craft heading for Sword beach. He was nineteen. 'As the tide went out, our craft sat on top of an anti-invasion mine, blowing a great hole in our starboard side.' There was nothing for it but to scramble ashore, dig a fox-hole and hope for the best as German warplanes strafed the beach. 'My thought at the time was, if I have to die it's not going to be in a hole. So back we went aboard our landing craft. I can still see the bodies on the beach and, later in the day, the planes releasing the gliders, the paratroops descending from the planes and some not opening, and us looking on helplessly.'

Sam Tuft of Brownhills waded ashore in the second wave as a private in the Queen's Royal Regiment on Gold Beach: 'The water was neck-deep. Your main concern was to keep your rifle dry. Things were chaotic, with artillery fire and sniping from hidden vantage points making it difficult to keep track of units. One of my first jobs after landing was to bury a fellow soldier, who had been badly blown up, in a field. The worst thing of all was talking and joking with your mates and then suddenly finding they weren't there.'

Fred Harvey of Pelsall went ashore on Juno Beach as a twenty-year-old gunner. 'A few miles offshore we stopped and a "Rhino" came into position to transfer us to shore. I remember thinking we were on our own now as we dashed for a position above the high-water mark. To our front was a concrete gun emplacement which had caused so much trouble, with two of the Canadian lads lying dead in front of the gun.'

Alan Rochelle, from Hednesford, landed at Sword Beach at noon. A sapper aged twenty with the Royal Engineers, he was charged with the task of unloading supply trucks. He went ashore in an LCI [landing craft infantry], a 160-foot long craft capable of carrying nearly 200 men, and its initial attempts at discharging its passengers nearly ended in disaster. 'There were parts of two companies on the LCI that I came in with. At first they tried to drop us too far out and the men who went out had to inflate their Mae Wests. They were floating and their feet didn't touch the ground. Some of the navy people on the craft jumped in to help them out. The LCI then pulled back and we put rope ladders down and were instructed to climb down into smaller assault craft to go ashore. We still got a wet landing but not as bad as the first lot. It was the first action I had seen. When I landed the assault troops had cleared much of the area but we were still under sniper and artillery fire. There weren't many German aircraft around but I remember one came along the beach trying to bomb the ships, but must have missed because I saw a spout of water come up. Another one flew along the beach and we all expected it to open fire on us, but it must have seen a better target further along. It was shot down as it got further along the beach. My biggest fear was stepping on a mine. Having a limb blown off, being maimed like that was terrifying. When the tanks came ashore I made sure that I only walked in their tracks, because I thought that if they hadn't set off I wasn't likely to. The beach was absolutely jam-packed with vehicles, all of them trying to get off the beach. We were at the beach longer than expected because we did not get inland as far as planned. Some of the ships off the beach were flying barrage balloons as the landings went on, but soon realised that the German artillery were using them to target the boats.'

As the infantry stormed the Normandy beaches companies of the Royal Engineers came ashore to clear the way for the massive build-up of vehicles and stores. Sapper Alan Jones of Dudley was twenty-four and it was his first day in action. Born and raised in Dudley, he was working in heavy engineering before being called up and was drafted in the Royal Engineers. He and his mates went ashore in landing craft with mine detectors and one of the great successes of the Second World War – Bailey bridges. A civilian engineer, Donald Bailey, had sketched out the basic details of his brainchild on the back of an envelope during a train journey. The Bailey bridge came into service in 1942 and became a legend; by the end of the war multiple Bailey bridges up to 1,000 feet long had been thrown across rivers from Britain to Burma. But the Engineers' job on D-Day, often under enemy fire, was to clear Nazi minefields and bolt shorter Bailey bridges into place across ditches and other obstacles. 'I remember feeling a bit scared. But we had a job to do, and that was that. The Bailey bridges were great. It was hard work but it was like a Meccano set.'

He recalls the satisfaction, by the end of the longest day, of seeing tanks and guns heading inland over his bridges as the Allies broke out from the beachhead.

For Bill Kendrick of Parkfield, Wolverhampton, D-Day brought a terrifying encounter with a fellow Black Countryman. Driving a Jeep converted to take stretchers, Private Kendrick was a veteran of Dunkirk, El Alamein and the Italian landings: 'I'd been on dozens of ships and landing craft before but D-Day was the only time I got seasick.' Storming ashore with the Green Howards on Gold Beach, he was sent forward to collect the wounded as bullets and shells scorched through the Normandy hedgerows. 'The infantry could drop into the trenches and there I was in my Jeep, sticking up like a great big wooden target. There were some of our tanks firing away in the next field and suddenly this bloody great Sherman came crashing through the hedge. I shouted, "Yow look where yoom shoving that tank," and he said, "Sorry mate, I dae see yow." I said, "Yowm from Wolverhampton, ain't yer?" Never did find out who he was.'

Having experienced several earlier retreats, the Jeep-ambulance driver half-expected another Dunkirk. But as the Allies drove hard inland German prisoners started pouring back. 'They were like a bunch of zombies, very pale, running down the road four abreast with no-one even guarding them. They were terrified and so was I. But at least they were getting out of it. We had to go forward.'

The sheer scale of D-Day stirred the emotions. Robert Simpson, an army medic from Warley, felt a lump in his throat at the sight of the massive Allied glider fleet passing overhead, and the terror of being strafed on the beach by German fighters. But his abiding memory was an act of humanity as two British soldiers seemed on the verge of killing a terrified German soldier: 'Our padre saved the German's life by persuading them to take him prisoner instead.'

Alf 'Tug' Wilson from Bloxwich was a glider pilot: 'We all knew it was dangerous. We knew they always aimed for the pilot. Kill the pilot and you've killed the glider. You felt pride in your regiment and pride in your army. But it was what you trained for and what you got paid for. We just wanted to get in there and do the job.'

His D-Day mission was to land his Horsa, carrying a gun, its Jeep and crew near the river Orne. Towed from Brize Norton to Normandy by a Halifax bomber, he cast off higher than planned and headed straight for Caen to lose speed and height. But a burst of anti-aircraft shells put a hole in his wing and he swung back, looking for a landing place among the dozens of gliders carpeting the Normandy meadows below. He chose his spot and was hedge-hopping towards it 30 feet up at 80 mph when he felt 'one hell of a bump'. A Horsa had crashed into him from above. As it shot past him the other glider, hinged in the centre for unloading, began to open up. Thankfully both gliders hit the ground and slewed to a halt without any injuries. The guns were unloaded and the heroes of the Glider Pilot Regiment made their way back to the invasion beaches. 'On the beach there were lines of British dead. I walked past to see if I knew anyone, but I didn't.'

Bob Stokes of Wednesfield, a private in the Oxfordshire & Buckinghamshire Light Infantry, arrived by Horsa glider in the late afternoon to defend a line 2 miles inland from Pegasus Bridge: 'We went into a ploughed field, nose-down, and the pilot was killed. A German anti-aircraft gun was shooting at us but couldn't shoot low enough. Someone took a bazooka and knocked it out, quite casually.'

Harry Anderson of Chapel Ash, Wolverhampton, was a veteran of the 1940 Dunkirk evacuation. On D-Day he was back in France as a lance corporal with the 4th/7th Royal Dragoon Guards. He landed on Gold Beach on the afternoon of D-Day. 'I always knew we would have to go back and finish off what we didn't do the first time. It had to be finished one way or the other. I just wanted to do the job and hoped I'd survive.'

He was a fitter, responsible for keeping the regiment's Sherman tanks rolling and repairing them if they broke down. But in the chaos of the beach landing only a few of the vehicles made it ashore. 'Even though we had been at Dunkirk, we didn't really know what to expect when we landed. There was a bit of resistance where we came ashore and there were an awful lot of Germans, but the big guns were keeping the Germans quiet. We did take some casualties, of course. Some men from my regiment are in the cemetery at Creully. All of the time there were a lot of shells falling and a lot of flak .Only a few of our tanks actually managed to get ashore, but it was only later in the day that we realised how many tanks we had lost during the day.'

Harry and his comrades moved away from the beach and headed towards the city of Caen, where they were held up by the German defenders. 'That evening I remember thinking about the men we had lost and that I was lucky to be alive.'

Jeff Pocock, of Penn, served with a recce unit, the Derbyshire Yeomanry, and endured hours of the 'continuous and overpowering' naval barrage before going ashore. The captain of the cargo ship *Winona* decided to beach the vessel at high tide. The Yeomanry's armoured cars were unloaded by cranes and the soldiers set foot on French soil by a most unglamorous means. 'We all thought we would go ashore from landing craft. In the event we ended up climbing down a wooden ladder. The scene was of utter devastation. Farmhouses had been wrecked, trees shattered and there were dead cattle in the fields.'

Ted Ford from Oxley, Wolverhampton, had a 'copy-book approach' at Juno Beach on the day after D-Day, on a landing craft delivering two armoured Weasels. 'But it turned out there was a pole under us which was used as sea defences. Either side of the pole were mines but luckily they didn't blow up. Wreckage was everywhere and with it dead bodies, some where they fell as they came ashore, others where they were blown up when their craft was hit.'

The build up continued and the danger increased. Geoff Ensor of Merry Hill, Wolverhampton, was a sub-lieutenant in the Royal Navy, bringing follow-up troops to the beaches forty-eight hours after the first landings. 'We went ashore on Sword Beach D+2. We should have been there on D-Day but didn't get the order. We were ferrying troops back and forward, often under fire. Eventually our ship, *Cap Tourane*, was hit by a German shell from the big guns at Le Havre. There were four of us writing home. Two went up on deck to see what was happening. When I went up the commander told me to deal with two dead bodies. One of them was our friend, Captain D.G. Thomas, Royal Marines, and I had to identify his body.'

Staffordshire Yeomanry and the Panzers
Allied planners had reckoned on losing up to 12,000 men on D-Day. In the event the Allies put 155,000 men ashore at a cost of about 2,500 lives, of whom more than 1,000 had died at Omaha. For some units D-Day had been a bloodbath. For many, keyed up to expect the worst, it

had almost been a walkover. It had proved a triumph of logistics, an operation that one officer likened to moving Birmingham across the Channel. But some of the hardest fighting of the war was to follow.There were still huge gaps in the Allied advance and historians can only guess what might have happened if the Germans had hit back harder. But the Germans took hours to decide that this really was the long-awaited invasion and that Normandy, not Calais, was the Allies' objective. When they finally attacked the German tanks were beaten off. Reuben Welsh of Brewood, a lance-sergeant in the Yeomanry, remembered the frustration of his regiment's tanks being held up on the crowded invasion beaches by 'blokes strolling around on the prom, like it was Blackpool'.

The Yeomanry managed to push inland where they met, and defeated, the only serious Nazi counter-attack of the day in a set-piece ambush. The Germans sent in fifty tanks and lost ten before withdrawing. The Yeomanry's commanding officer, Lieutenant-Colonel Jim Eadie, had predicted the Nazi move a month earlier and planned his ambush, supported by field guns. Reuben Welsh recalls: 'Our right flank tank was commanded by Sergeant Les Joyce, a gamekeeper before the war on Lord Dartmouth's estate at Patshull. Les had a good eye for country and vision like a hawk. He knocked out the three leading tanks with three shots. The rest panicked and veered off north where our B Squadron knocked out a further four. I believe that we saved the day. Our thin red line held and they never came again.'

After the war, a German commander testified to the British shooting. 'Just as I feared, the Allies had occupied all the strategic positions,' said Wilhelm von Gottberg, group commander of 22 Panzer Regiment. 'Ten of my tanks were knocked out by the British even before their tanks were within our firing range. We had to give up. I am still convinced that had we been given orders to attack during the early hours of the invasion we would have succeeded in throwing the enemy back into the sea. But there was nothing I could do except curse the short-sightedness of my own high command.'

Night falls

As the longest day slipped slowly into night thousands of Commandos, paras, gunners, tank crews and infantrymen dug themselves into slit trenches in the orchards and meadows of the bocage (the lightly wooded countryside so typical of northern France) and grabbed what sleep they could. Bill Bennett, unaware his bravery had earned him a mention in dispatches, recalls the evening. Worn out, he and his colleagues were too exhausted to think about what they had achieved as they rested on their ship. 'We were so tired. We had tried to sleep on the way over but we couldn't, and we had been up working all day so we just went to sleep.

Ninety-five-year-old Clarice Onions holds the tobacco tin presented to her father
for service in the First World War
[see page 3]

Clarice's father (seated) was assigned to the 'trench police' on the Western Front.   [see page 3]

Alvin Smith: 'Would you love me if I was a soldier?'
[see page 11]

Picking up the dead – Percy 'Ginger' Best on the right.
[see page 13]

Cecil Rhodes in advance of the Dunkirk landings of 1940.
[see page 28]

Cecil Rhodes displays his Dunkirk medal.
[see page 28]

Tony Southall, survivor of the surrender at Kalamata.
[see page 34]

Adrian Sammerlaan – 'One of our planes is missing', 1943.
[see page 43]

Adrian Sammerlaan at the time of writing.
[see page 43]

Jim Chapman experienced the 'death' of a Lancaster bomber in 1944.
[see page 46]

Keeping the memory alive: Jim Chapman today.
[see page 46]

Facing the reality of D-Day in 1944: Ken Leighfield.
[see page 62]

Ken Leighfield salutes his fallen comrades at the Jerusalem Cemetery in Bayeux. [see page 62]

Jim Klyn and his resistance comrades undermined the Nazis in every way they could. [see page 85]

Having experienced unimaginable horrors as a Japanese POW, Ron Walker had
more reason than most to celebrate VJ Day.
[see page 97]

Ron Walker: 'If anyone had told me that I'd still be around sixty years later…'
[see page 97]

In Memory of the 70 people
who lost their lives in the
underground explosion at
Fauld Munitions Store,
near Burton upon Trent,
27th November 1944

Memorial plaque for the Fauld Munitions Store.
[see page 88]

John Owen as a teenager aboard HMS *Alamein* in 1956.
[see page 107]

Veteran of the Suez 'Crisis': John Owen today.
[see page 107]

Nineteen-year-old National Serviceman John Bentley was soon to exchange the barracks at Bloxwich for snipers in Port Said.
[see page 107]

Paul Stokes revisits 'The Hole' in 2005.
[see page 116]

Dean Jenkins recalls the mayhem at Goose Green in 1982.
[see page 123]

'At the time you feel nothing. It was all about survival.' Chris Pollard recalls the sinking of HMS *Coventry*. [see page 127]

But I do remember that my impression of that night was of tremendous noise, with all the guns and bombs, as well as hundreds of planes, and the smell of the cordite.'

Alan Rochelle, the sapper from Hednesford, recalls that morale among the men that evening was good. 'I remember being thankful that I had made it, and I thought about those who hadn't. During the day I had been with the others and been too busy to stop and think, but at night in a little trench with all the bangs and flashes going off overhead you suddenly wonder where everyone had gone, and that did feel a bit lonely. You can't appreciate what it must have been like for these men. So many lives were lost. It makes me very proud.'

Lorry driver Len Whitehouse recalls: 'There was a bit of a celebration on the evening and I remember filling up with tears a bit and moving away from the party. I said a little prayer for the lads who didn't make it.'

Aftermath
The original first-day target for Operation Overlord was to seize the city of Caen and a huge swathe of land around it. In the event only a fraction of this territory was taken. By midnight British and American forces should have linked up along the full length of the invasion coast. They had not.

D-Day ended with the Germans in disarray. In the west the Americans had enjoyed the best and worst of the day. The landing at Utah Beach had gone well but the survivors of 'Bloody Omaha' were exhausted and shattered by the experience. For the British and Canadians further east, the day had been a hard-fought success. For some units D-Day had been a bloodbath. For many, keyed up to expect the worst, it had been almost a walkover. But the hardest fighting of the war was to follow.

By nightfall on D-Day the first British and German wounded were already back in hospital in England. Joan Onions of Short Heath, Wolverhampton, was twenty-seven and a trainee nurse at Leicester Royal Infirmary when it was taken over by the military. She was called on to tend to the Operation Overlord casualties. 'We weren't officially told what was going on but it was obvious something important was happening because the military took over everything and all the other patients were evacuated. The first convoys arrived during the night, the conditions of the soldiers were assessed and then they were sent on to the right departments – such as shell shock, shrapnel wounds and rheumatic conditions due to being outside for a long time. Many suffered stomach problems due to swallowing sea water that was contaminated with blood and oil. Those poor lads were in a bad way; they had to have their stomachs pumped constantly. But one of the things I will never forget is the soldiers who had been given sabotaged bottles of wine to drink. German sympathisers pretended to welcome them, slapped them on the back and said, "Thank you, Tommy, you saved us," and of course the lads drank them down gladly after what they had been through. But the bottles were laced with acid and it burnt their mouths, throats and stomachs. Those wounds were horrific. But the job satisfaction was terrific. I can't remember what I did yesterday but I can remember what I did on D-Day as clearly as anything.'News of the D-Day success spread around the world within hours. Prisoner of war Thomas Parton of Willenhall heard about the D-Day landing from a radio hidden in a medicine ball at a German POW camp: 'I knew there was light at the end of the tunnel when I heard that message.'

In Normandy the Germans had a sleepless night, drawing up their own battle plans. The tightly hedged bocage, with small fields and many copses and orchards, was ideal for a defensive battle. No Allied soldier who served in the Normandy campaign will forget the whine of German multiple rocket launchers or the devastating effect of the feared 88mm gun. Snipers were everywhere. A few days into the campaign a rifle cracked and Ernie Barker fell dying. He served in the Somerset Light Infantry. His best mate was Bill Baron of Wolverhampton, who remembers his fallen comrade as 'a really good bloke. Two young boys arrived to make up some of our losses. They were obviously very bewildered and scared. I vividly remember Ernie saying, "Come here, lads, and I'll make you a cup of tea."' As Ernie brewed up a cuppa for the new lads the sniper fired. The battle for Normandy was won hedgerow by hedgerow, skirting fields littered with the stiff, rot-swollen bodies of cows. The Germans made constant counter-attacks. Time after time British gunners saved the day. Ken Reynolds of Hednesford went ashore after D-Day as a bombardier with a battery of big guns. He recalls the back-breaking effort of shifting a battery of massive howitzers up to four times a day through the dense Normandy countryside. In one memorable barrage during the attack codenamed Epsom, 400 guns in his artillery group opened fire on the same target, a German headquarters. Four hundred shells crashed into the target, followed two minutes later by another 400. As the gunners went forward they saw the awesome result of their work. 'Nearly every shell hole covered the next shell hole. We found Germans wandering around who had been sent completely mad. They were just out of it.'

Arthur Cooper from Pelsall also served with the big guns. But nothing, he says, compared with the firepower of the Royal Navy ships offshore which could fire 10 or 15 miles inland. The express-train roar of their massive shells was 'music to the ears' of the Brits. Further inland,

Gunner/Signaller Cooper watched his howitzers smashing up German attacks: 'The muzzles of the guns used to get red hot. On one occasion the muzzle of one gun blew away, narrowly missing the head of the CO. There was a direct hit on one of our gun pits, killing nine members of the gun team, the second-in-command and the battery major, who happened to be in the gun pit at the time. One night, during an enemy counter-attack, a shell exploded on the side of our gun pit, seriously wounding an NCO who was standing right in front of me. The whole area stank to death and the stench coming from rotting carcasses of dead cattle in the fields was revolting. I shall never forget that awful smell.'

It was not until 19 August that the Allied armies finally encircled and trapped the Germans at the Falaise Gap. The scale of the defeat was staggering. Some ten thousand Germans were killed at Falaise and fifty thousand taken prisoner. Hitler had begun the campaign in June with fifty divisions in Normandy; by the end of August barely ten were left capable of fighting. Total German losses in the Normandy campaign of 6 June to 29 August were about two hundred thousand killed and wounded and about the same number taken prisoner. The US Army suffered 20,838 killed, the British Army (including Canadian, Poles and others) 15,995. The RAF and USAAF each lost about eight thousand. As the Germans fled eastwards, pursued by Allied armies and savaged by Allied air forces, the roads of France were left choked with blazing and abandoned Nazi vehicles. 'It was literally possible', Eisenhower wrote grimly, 'to walk for hundreds of yards at a time, stepping on nothing but dead and decaying flesh.' Vast tracts of France were simply abandoned to the Allies. Yet the war was by no means over. As fresh British troops were poured into Europe the D-Day invasion beaches left an indelible and sobering impression on all who crossed them.

Frank Spittle of Wolverhampton would never claim to be a Normandy veteran. He was an ambulance driver with the King's Own Scottish Borderers and came ashore weeks after D-Day on his way to the bloody battles of Walcheren and the Rhine Crossing. 'We landed at Arromanches Mulberry harbour in Jeeps. The fighting was over but we could see hundreds of fresh graves. We could see what was coming for us.'

The Germans had yet to launch their surprise winter attack known as the Battle of the Bulge and the Allied attempt to speed up the assault on Germany was to end in the tragedy of Arnhem. The bloody crossing of the Rhine was almost a year away, and every yard closer to Germany seemed to bring more fanatical resistance. Yet the momentum that started on the beaches of Gold, Juno, Sword, Omaha and Utah could not be halted. D-Day, 6 June 1944, was a turning point of the war.

Bayeux tailpiece

For Dennis Bateman, a twenty-five-year-old corporal, the Normandy invasion brought a special place in history. After the invasion he and his crew of the Royal Electrical & Mechanical Engineers spent a month recovering shattered vehicles from the invasion beaches and inland. It was wearing, dangerous work as German snipers and long-range artillery took their daily toll. But during a quiet spell, about a month after D-Day, Corporal Bateman was given a day off. He went to Bayeux Cathedral. 'I'm not a religious man,' he explains at his home in Kinver, 'but I wanted to give thanks for still being alive.' As he prayed he noticed three old French men unravelling what looked like a roll of wallpaper. 'I can see them now. They were draping it over the church chairs, as if they were putting it out to dry. I couldn't make out what they were saying in French but I went closer and could see that it was a tapestry.'

It was years later that Mr Bateman realised he had stumbled across the priceless nine hundred-year-old Bayeux Tapestry, commemorating the Norman invasion of England in 1066. During the war the tapestry had been hidden to keep it safe from Allied bombing and Nazi pilferers. 'In 1991 I went back to Bayeux on a sort of pilgrimage. I found the graves of three old pals and went to see the tapestry. They really gave me the VIP treatment. One of the women in charge said I must have been the first British person to have seen the tapestry after the war. It was an honour. But it was just a question of being in the right place at the right time.' *May 1994*

Kohima

He cannot forget the beaten Japs. His comfortable home is another world from the mud and filth of Kohima and yet the sights still haunt him. Sick, starving, disease-ridden and shell-shocked, the Japanese cowered in ditches and craters, too weak even to commit ritual suicide. These were the fragments of the 'invincible' forces of Imperial Japan after it had tangled with the British 14th Army – the so-called 'Forgotten Army'. In June 1944, British and Indian troops, having linked up at milestone 108 on the road between Imphal and Kohima in north-east India, were inflicting the worst defeat suffered by Japanese forces in the Second World War. And yet the great battle of Kohima and Imphal is barely remembered. The deeds of the soldiers who fought there were overshadowed in 1944 by the D-Day landings and their commemoration, fifty years on, was drowned out by the D-Day anniversary. 'We were the "Forgotten Army" then and we're the "Forgotten Army" now,' says the old sergeant, tanned, fit and still ramrod straight for all the advancing years. He served in a Territorial battalion of the Worcesters, one of the units of raw, astonished young British and Indian Army forces rushed into battle as the Japanese Army began its drive from Burma into India in April, 1944. They were anxious days. The Japanese, by a formidable blend of discipline, junglecraft and terrorism of the civilian population, had built a huge empire. Three years earlier they had defeated the great British stronghold of Singapore and gone on to occupy half of Asia. As they thrust over the Indian border the Japanese laid siege to the garrison at Imphal and drove on to Kohima, a cool and pretty hill station comprising the district commissioner's bungalow, a motor depot, a hospital and not much else. At Kohima the Japanese finally met their match.'It was a bloody awful, vicious battle. At one stage the enemies were dug in just 25 yards apart at opposite ends of the commissioner's tennis court. It was more like the First World War than the Second, fought mainly by the infantry from dug-outs and trenches. And it was fought over hills, like the Long Mynd only covered in trees. The hills had been cut into terraces and the Japs were dug in. Imagine attacking over that lot. I remember we spent one entire day hauling a tank up a slope by hand so that it could fire on a Jap bunker.'No-one who fought in the sixty-four-day battle of Kohima will forget it. The monsoon-drenched battlefield was a nightmarish landscape of mud, craters and tree stumps. Whole forests were swept away by artillery barrages, hillsides littered with rotting corpses. But this was not the British Army that had surrendered so meekly at Singapore. The 14th Army, led by the legendary General Bill Slim, had learned the art of jungle warfare. 'Very strong and well disciplined', a Japanese officer noted of the British 2nd Infantry Division. The Brits fought in plimsolls, dropped by parachute. On one memorable night they infiltrated an entire brigade of 2,500 men, single file and silent, through the Japanese lines. And when the British, having broken the siege on Kohima, went on the offensive, they fought like lions. The 'invincible' Japanese were pushed back, often at bayonet point, and with the aid of some ancient, obsolete equipment.

'That's why we first called ourselves the "Forgotten Army". We were a cast-off army with second-hand tanks and old guns. All the best kit was in Italy and Normandy. Whenever you read anything about the war in those days it was all North Africa, Italy and northern France, never us, for all the viciousness of the fighting, the appalling conditions and the disease.' The Worcesters, eight hundred strong at the start of the battle, lost three hundred men, 'and we thought we'd got out of it lightly'.The Japanese casualties were appalling. Their 35th Division attacked Kohima fifteen thousand strong. Only four hundred survived.Yet there was no sympathy for the beaten enemy. 'You may hear soldiers say that the Germans were first-class soldiers. But the Japs, well, we couldn't find any compassion for them. That's how I feel even to this day. They were vicious and nasty. Their bravery was magnificent but their logistics were poor and they ended up starving to death. I can see them now at the end of the fighting, Japs crawling in shell holes and irrigation ditches, too weak even to kill themselves. They had to send an officer out with the patrols, to make sure the men brought the Japs back as prisoners instead of . . .' The sentence is unfinished, the meaning quite clear. After Kohima the 14th Army pushed on past Imphal and across the plains of Burma. They inflicted half a million casualties on the Japanese. Hollywood later spread the lie that the Yanks beat the Japs, but what saddened the 14th Army was that their own country virtually ignored their achievement. As Britain celebrated VE Day the 14th Army was still slogging it out with the retreating Japanese. The sergeant and his mates were resigned to a long and bloody invasion of the Japanese mainland when, one day in August 1945, word came through that a special sort of bomb had been dropped at a place called Hiroshima and it was all over. At Kohima they erected a memorial to the 2nd Division with the legend: 'When you go home, tell them of us – and say/For their tomorrow we gave our today'.Something is missing from this interview. No names, no pack drill, as they used to say. The old sergeant remembers and is proud to share his memories, but he would be 'deeply embarrassed' to see his name in print when no-one spares a thought for the ones who didn't come home. The old soldiers of the 'Forgotten' 14th Army wear their nickname with pride. Forgotten then, forgotten now, but proud of the battles they fought and the mates they left behind. *June 1994*

The 'Forgotten Army'

Mud, leeches, mosquitoes and monsoon. Kohima was hell even before the bullets started flying. As the world rejoiced at the Normandy Landings in June 1944, it seemed no-one had a second thought for the British lads fighting 2,000 miles to the east. As a result, the world seems to think that it was the Americans alone who defeated the Japanese Empire. It was not. The Japanese Army was fought to a standstill, turned back from the gates of India and finally routed by Les Greenow and a few thousand like him, and driven back through Burma.

'I'm not bitter about the D-Day celebrations,' he stresses at his home in Wolverley near Kidderminster. 'Those chaps had a devil of a job to do. But they had a lot of heavy stuff with them. We were on our own. The battle of Kohima went on night after night, day after day. You could never say, we've done it – let's rest. What I remember is the persistence, and the comradeship. The terrain was terrible. You'd climb 400 feet and then have to go up another 400. Everything happened at short range.' Les Greenow praises the courage of the local Naga people who acted as guides and stretcher bearers and the endurance of his mates, fighting in conditions when even staying alive was a challenge. A medic corporal with the Worcestershire Regiment, he remembers burying a sergeant whose hand wound he had dressed only a few days before. He recalls the heroic young officer who sent for a flamethrower to help attack a Japanese machine-gun nest. Impatient, he decided to have a go himself and was killed. There was not enough left of him to bury.

While the Normandy campaign was stuffed with tanks and big guns, Britain's 14th Army in Burma got hand-me-down weapons and barely a change of uniform from Kohima to Rangoon. 'And we never had any war reporters out with us. If anyone had ever said you're going to walk all the way to Rangoon, I'd have said I'm going home. But we did it – 700 miles. I was so proud.' *June 2004*

The Chindits

As Les Greenow and his colleagues were pushing the Japanese back in Burma, the legendary Chindits were causing mayhem behind enemy lines. It was a curious war. Bill Williams was a young South Staffordshire Regiment officer in a Dakota transport aircraft with five men – and five mules. They landed 200 miles in the Japanese rear on a makeshift airstrip scraped out of a paddyfield by 'calfdozers' flown in by glider the day before. It was the first time mules had been flown into combat. Bill Williams recalls his conversation with a soldier as their aircraft came in to land.'This is bloody dangerous, isn't it, sir?' asked the squaddie.'Yes, it is,' replied the officer.

'Oh well, I suppose they know what they're doing.'The Chindits, named after Chinthe, a mythical Burmese creature symbolising protection, were created by the legendary Orde Wingate, a British general who never accepted the common view that the Japanese were invincible jungle fighters.

'At first we regarded the Japanese with terror,' admits Bill Williams, of Claverley, near Wolverhampton. 'There was this automatic assumption that they were going to invade India.'

On a high ridge near the landing zone, the South Staffs proved otherwise. Surprised by a Japanese company above them, they charged and routed them. In this battle of Pagoda Hill, another officer, Lieutenant George Cairns, won a posthumous VC, fighting on even after his left arm was severed by a Japanese sword.

Cyril Baldock of Lower Penn, Wolverhampton, was a lieutenant in a Chindit reconnaissance unit. He went into action on foot, leading his men and mules 500 miles over mountains 8,000 feet high to attack a Japanese garrison. It went badly. Exhausted, dehydrated and fighting in temperatures of 100F, the Brits were beaten back. He recalls one image of hell when flamethrowers were loaded on mules and sent forward for an attack: 'An incendiary bullet went straight through the flamethrower setting it and the mule on fire. It rushed around causing absolute carnage.'But the worst fate for a Chindit was to be wounded. With no means of evacuating casualties, Cyril's column had to leave them behind, either to be killed by the advancing Japanese or to commit suicide. 'They were left with the means to do it,' he recalls. 'It was a horrible thing to have to do. These were men you had played rugby with or been sitting with in the mess. It was awful.'

And yet by the end of 1944 the 'Forgotten Army' had almost defeated the Japanese. British soldiers, properly trained, led and supplied from the air, were better than anything Japan could throw against them.'Despite everything,' says Bill Williams, 'I remember this tremendous feeling of confidence. I can't remember anyone ever questioning whether this was a clever thing to do. The leadership, all the way down from Wingate to the NCOs, was fantastic. The men were tough, hard-nosed chaps.' After being overseas for five years he was evacuated from Burma with a mortar wound and suffering from malaria, jaundice and dysentery. Cyril Baldock came out leading a party of sick and wounded before being flown back to India.

In early June 1944 Bill Williams was recovering from his wound and jungle diseases in an Indian hospital when a brother officer came into the ward with news of D-Day in far-off Normandy. He remarked, 'Now the "Forgotten Army" will never be remembered.' *June 2004*

Death in the jungle
In the sweating, steaming jungle night all hell broke loose. Jim Jones thought he would never see the next day. His band of a dozen soldiers had sneaked across a railway bridge over a river in Burma. Their job was to hold this fragile bridgehead until reinforcements arrived. Suddenly the Japanese counter-attacked in a tornado of air-bursting shells, bombs and machine-gun fire. A grenade exploded in Jim's trench. Two of his mates fell wounded. He grabbed the Bren gun, opened fire and cut down the swarming Japanese. The line held. Jim Jones was a hero.

He had joined the Army in 1940 as a sixteen-year-old grocer's boy from Warley. He stood just 5 foot 4 inches tall, weighed 9 stone and was, he grins, 'young and daft'. In the living room of his home in Oldbury he recalls, 'I lied about my age. The recruiting sergeant said I should go for a little walk and come back when I was eighteen.'

If his parents were horrified they hid it well. He remembers his mother saying, 'If he wants to get his bloody head blown off, let him.'

Six years later he came home as Sergeant Jones MM, a veteran soldier and all of twenty-two. He was awarded the Military Medal for that desperate night's fighting in Burma. Did he feel brave at the time? 'It was just self-preservation. I had to encourage the men because if we packed in we were finished. The Japs didn't recognise white flags. But after it was over I thought, how the hell didn't I die? I never expected to live.'The official citation says: 'L/Cpl Jones was in command of the sector manning this part of the perimeter. His personal behaviour was magnificent. He remained cool and collected throughout. In spite of the noise he could clearly be heard giving orders and encouragement to his men. His bearing was an example to all.'Jim Jones was part of the 'Forgotten Army'. While all eyes were on the dazzling D-Day invasion of France, the lads in Burma counted their bloody victories in yards of shattered jungle. Says Jim, 'Someone told us the Japs would be little blokes with glasses. The first one I saw was 6 foot, very big and dead.' In the epic battle of Kohima, he adds, the Japanese were as close as the house over the road, no more than 30 yards away. 'They'd fire like hell at us, and we'd roll grenades back at them.'

It was a filthy, merciless war. When you have seen British prisoners of war lashed to trees with barbed wire through their mouths, he says, you do not forgive. He talks with satisfaction of the time he and his pals spotted the Japanese forming up for an attack. His team opened fire and killed at least a hundred. Such sights can do terrible things to the human mind. Did he suffer nightmares?

'Not real nightmares. But when I first came home I kept thinking I could see these dead bodies at the bottom of the garden. I thought the police would be coming after me because I shouldn't have killed them. Sometimes it seems just like yesterday and we're scurrying down the jungle track and ambushing the Japs. I can hear the screams.'

Jim Jones and his mates formed a local branch of the Burma Star Association, named after their campaign medal. They met once a week to chew the fat. But the years took their toll. The numbers dwindled from thirty to eight. The standard of the West Bromwich Branch of the Burma Star Association was laid up at St Andrew's Church, Carters Green. The branch, of which he is chairman, is wound up.

A sad moment? For the first time in this chat the old soldier's eyes glisten as his wife, Doris, looks across and offers to make some tea.

'It is sad. But half the lads are sick and some of the others were having to change buses twice to get to meetings. The decision was taken.'

Some years ago he and Doris made a pilgrimage to Kohima. He barely recognised the place. The tennis court, scene of the bitterest fighting, is preserved as a war memorial but someone had built a beautiful new bungalow over his old slit trench. Nearby stands the Kohima Memorial. Jim Jones says his little band of Burma Star veterans will keep in touch, if only to arrange each other's funerals. He suddenly chuckles with the graveyard humour of old soldiers everywhere: 'I'll have to hurry up and die or there will be no-one left to bury me.' *March 2003*

To Arnhem

The D-Day landings of 6 June 1944 had been a bigger success than anyone dared to hope. Three months later the Germans were in full retreat across France. Suddenly the Allies saw a chance to seize three bridges in Holland, outflank the Nazis and win the war in a matter of weeks. But the third bridge was a bridge too far . . . In the pitch-darkness, no more than 6 feet away, a motor-cycle combination suddenly appeared. 'It came right up to the trench I was in,' recalls George Green. 'I thought, bloody hell, what's this? Then they started jabbering away in German.' The twenty-five-year-old para cocked his Sten gun, jumped up and blazed away. But after a few shots, the notoriously unreliable Sten jammed. It was his turn to dash for safety as bullets flew around him. 'No-one believed me. But the next morning there was the motorbike with bullet holes in it.'

George Green, of Tettenhall, was defending the perimeter, holding the ever-diminishing British line as the Germans ruthlessly stamped out the bold but ill-planned Arnhem offensive. Five days after parachuting into Arnhem George was one of the lucky ones who escaped. Arnhem became a byword for courage, muddle and tragedy. Of the 10,005 members of 1st Airborne Division dropped by parachute and glider at Arnhem fewer than 2,500 returned unhurt. Almost 1,200 were killed. The rest, more than 6,000, were missing, wounded or captured. Codenamed Operation Market Garden, it was the brainchild of the legendary Monty, Field Marshal Bernard Montgomery. His aim was a three-pronged airborne assault to grab three bridges in the Dutch towns of Grave, Nijmegen and Arnhem. The Americans would seize the first two, with the British taking the bridge over the Rhine at Arnhem. As the paras and glider-borne infantry held the bridges a huge Allied force of tanks would storm northwards towards them. The plan was to sweep past the Germans' heavily defended Siegfried Line, open a 'back door' into the heart of Germany and end the war in a matter of weeks.

The American part of the plan worked brilliantly, but the British attack on Arnhem was doomed from the outset. Instead of landing on the crucial bridge, the gliders and paratroops were dropped up to 8 miles from the town centre and had to fight their way through. Instead of one mighty assault the troops arrived over a period of days, giving the Germans plenty of time to counter-attack. Instead of finding the town lightly defended, the British ran into two battered but defiant German divisions with tanks. New radios refused to work. Allied supplies were dropped into German hands. The British Guards Armoured Division, instead of dashing boldly forward to Arnhem, became bogged down. The operation began on 17 September 1944. Nine days later the last of the defeated British troops slipped across the river to safety. But on that bright, sunny Sunday when George Green and Jack Baker of the First Battalion of the Parachute Regiment climbed aboard their Dakota aircraft in Lincolnshire, the mood was electric. 'It was such a relief,' says Jack Baker, of Sedgley. 'Before Arnhem we'd had fifteen operations planned and then cancelled. 'We were fed up,' agrees George. 'We wanted to get in there.' But not everyone was so eager for the fray. In the days before the attack Harold Pugh of Wolverhampton and his mates in the South Staffordshire Regiment's crack glider-borne Second Battalion had slept on the cold, wet floor of an RAF hangar. In his view they were in no condition to fight. 'We had been indoctrinated. They'd told us we'd be up against a few Waffen SS and some old-crock soldiers. One of our officers even packed his best uniform and pyjamas!' But even before their Horsa gliders took off in the first wave, Harold Pugh and others in the South Staffs had heard whispers that all was not well. 'We knew that the new radios weren't working. Someone reported it to the higher-ups but they were told they couldn't rock the boat now.

'The South Staffs' gliders landed, or crashed, in meadows 8 miles from Arnhem to secure the dropping zones for the much bigger parachute assault. 'We knew something was wrong,' recalls Harold. 'We started to take casualties within ten minutes from mortars and machine-guns. We were so far away from Arnhem I don't think the Germans even realised we were after the bridge.' The paras arrived minutes later in a massive daylight drop and began fighting their way into Arnhem. 'It was a beautiful day, just like an exercise,' says Jack Baker. But it soon became a nightmare. Forced off the main roads by German armoured cars, the paras had to slog through endless terraced gardens. Every corner, every shed, became a German strongpoint.

'We took the first bang after about three hours,' recalls George Green. 'Four of our blokes were killed straight away. One was set on fire by his own phosphorous bomb. We tried to help him but we couldn't, because his ammunition was exploding. It was terrible.' The Paras' Second Battalion, meanwhile, was moving quickly forward. Lightly armed, they seized the bridge and held on grimly. 'It was heavy going and we took a lot of casualties,' says Jack Dawson, of Penn. 'Our job was to hold the bridge until the other battalions came.' But they never came. And nor did the advancing British armoured column. 'We were expecting tanks. Every time we heard the clank of tracks we were told they're ours until you see otherwise.' But all the tanks were German. For reasons which have never been explained, British top brass had ignored warnings from the Dutch Resistance that two German divisions were in the area. Against odds like that there was only one option. 'There were twelve of us,' says Jack Baker. 'We ran into five Tiger tanks and a flame-thrower. Our officer capitulated. The Germans were gleeful. They snatched off our red berets and stamped on them. Then it was just a question of shuffling off.' Harold Pugh was captured but cannot remember the details. 'There is a void for two days. I can't remember what happened. Either I did something bad or someone did bad things to me.' Jack Dawson was captured on the Thursday morning. It was a wretched experience. 'We had been told to fight our way back to Oosterbeek. We were hiding in the rubble but we had no ammo and they just picked us up. It is a very tricky business, surrendering. The front-line German soldiers were OK but the others knocked you around a bit.' For Jack Dawson, Jack Baker and Harold Pugh, the great adventure at Arnhem ended in a nightmarish VE Day rail journey, crammed fifty to a cattle truck, to the POW camps in Germany. For George Green it meant the bitter, bloody last stand at Oosterbeek, finally slipping across the river to safety at dead of night as the fighting ebbed. 'I think it was the rain that saved us more than anything. The Germans hated it as much as we did.' The four old soldiers remember the affection, and help, they got from brave Dutch families whose quiet little town was suddenly pitched into hell on a peaceful weekend fifty years ago. 'It was shocking, going in on a Sunday,' says Harold Pugh, his medals lightly clinking as he shakes his head in regret. 'You shouldn't do something like that on a Sunday.' *September 1994*

If only we'd had bazookas
It was the lull before the storm. Bill Hewitt was a twenty-three-year-old private in the 2nd Battalion of the South Staffordshire Regiment, a crack airborne unit that went to war in gliders. At his home in Sutton Coldfield he recalls the tragedy of a battle that had not been thought through. 'The leaders were all so keen to go and we'd been told nine times the job was on and then off. There was one officer who didn't want us to go because tanks had been seen in the area. He was sent on sick leave. On the Sunday morning we were marched out to the aerodrome and it was a magnificent sight to see all those gliders and planes.'

Private Hewitt, part of a mortar team, sat down hard in the Horsa glider. His seat strut punched a hole straight through the glider's skin, a reminder of how flimsy these great machines were. The South Staffs took off at 10.30am and made a perfect landing 8 miles from Arnhem at 1.30pm. 'It was very quiet, so quiet that I walked back to the glider to collect my sandwiches. We knew the paras were doing well and Colonel Frost had taken the bridge. The next morning, the Monday, we set off to help Frost. But our officer decided not to go any further until the next morning when the other half of the battalion was coming. It was the worst thing we could possibly have done.' Instead of making a dash for the bridge, the five hundred lean, fit men of the South Staffords dug in for a second night. The German defenders had time to organise. The rest is history. The next day the column passed a knocked-out Tiger tank. 'I remember looking at this huge thing and thinking, how do you deal with that with a 3-inch mortar? The next thing someone warned us that a tank was coming.'

The Black Country lads took cover in a dell but the German tank cruised around, firing at will. As scores of his mates died or surrendered, Bill Hewitt and a mate made a dash back to the British positions at Oosterbeek. But the sharp, offensive battle planned by the top brass had turned into a gruelling siege by overwhelming German forces. On the Thursday Bill was wounded in the chin by a mortar bomb. Out of action, he was sent to work with the wounded until the victorious Germans arrived. He says he was well treated in captivity. But for his young bride, Emma, there were weeks of agony until the official telegram arrived on 7 December 1944 – their son Paul's first birthday – with the news that Private Hewitt was a prisoner, believed wounded. 'My weight went down to six stone,' she recalls. 'My dad said, better buck up or there'll be nothing left of you when he comes home.' In the lawless chaos of defeated Germany, Bill Hewitt and his mates fled westward in a succession of stolen cars, finally bartering a limousine for a flight home. He has strong views on the doomed operation. 'The fighting was magnificent,' he says, 'but the planning was atrocious. Why did we land 8 miles from the bridge? Why not right on top of it, like we did on D-Day?' He still wonders what might have been, if only the Brits could have fought off the German tanks. 'It was a bridge too far but it needn't have been, if it had been thought through correctly. If we'd had bazookas instead of mortars it would have been wonderful. But it was too stupid for words.' *September 2004*

The glider pilot's story
With no engine and 10 tons of glider, gun and soldiers to control, there was only one chance of a landing at Arnhem.'We were the third to land,' recalls Geoff Higgins at his home in Stourbridge. 'The first one landed all right but the second one turned over. The co-pilot was killed. We had to get down behind this glider and we landed, bump, bump, but apart from that there was no trouble. And, of course, it was a lovely day.'

Everyone who flew into battle at Arnhem on Sunday 17 September 1944 remembers the beautiful blue sky of a sunny autumn day. They also remember the early mood of optimism. Did he share that confidence? 'Oh, yes. You have to remember what the gliders had done on D-Day only a short time before. They were marvellous and some of the glider pilots were back at their bases in England within three days. The motto of the Glider Pilot Regiment was 'nothing is impossible' and we thought Arnhem was going to be as easy as D-Day, when our squadron only lost one man.'

Geoff's war had begun in May 1940. He was studying in London to become a teacher when he was called up and posted to a tank regiment, the Fife & Forfar Yeomanry. Bored after three years' training in Britain, he applied for a transfer. His first application, to the SAS, was torn up by his commanding officer. His second choice was the Glider Pilot Regiment. It was an elite army unit, offering excitement, flying qualifications and more pay. A few weeks later he was learning the basics of flight in a Tiger Moth biplane before graduating to Hamilcars, the biggest gliders ever used in combat.

On the first day of the Arnhem attack thirteen Hamilcars went into action carrying light tanks and other vehicles. Geoff's payload was a formidable 19-pound anti-tank gun and its crew. His orders were to stay with the gun until he could be withdrawn back to Britain, probably within forty-eight hours. At first, after that hairy landing, everything went to plan. The gunners set up their weapon at a strategic corner covering the main road to Utrecht. 'Everything seemed to be going very well. We heard a lot of shouting and banging and we were told the lads had taken the bridge. Everything seemed fine and we carried on defending the perimeter. But after three days we began to realise there were a lot of Germans about.'

There was a sudden whirlwind of shells and mortar bombs. The anti-tank gun was knocked out without firing a shot. Its supply truck went up in a cloud of smoke and flames. 'We were fighting an enemy we couldn't see. It was just shells and bangs and, being in a slit trench by yourself, you are all alone.' So alone, in fact, that when the inevitable British retreat began, Geoff Higgins was not told. He peeked over his slit trench to see a couple of British stragglers in the dark. 'One of them said, "we're getting out – take hold of my coat tails." So I did and we joined this queue.' At the front of the queue, unseen by the surrounding Germans, hundreds of British troops were slipping to safety over the Rhine. 'But when dawn came up, well, it was all over. Suddenly we were surrounded by Germans and they were very aggressive and excitable.' Some soldiers describe being taken prisoner as a desolate and demoralising experience. Geoff Higgins is not so sure. 'When you've gone through two or three days of shelling, well, it could be a relief. You know you can't do anything more.'

As the British prisoners were marched into Arnhem, he recalls the smiling faces of Tiger tank crews lined up on the road. 'They seemed really cheerful. They were just very happy to see us and they handed out some of the cigarettes that had been dropped by parachute for us, and missed. I'll never forget one of them giving me a Player's cigarette.'

He spent the rest of the war in German POW camps, returning home in June 1945. With years of hindsight how does this one-time glider pilot reflect on the tragedy of Arnhem? Was it a crazy gamble? 'I still think that it should have come off. The Airborne did everything that was asked of them. They went straight to the bridge, took it and held it. The armoured column should have reached us but didn't. It's the Dutch people I feel sorry for. I try to go back every year, and I have to tell them that we left them in a bigger mess than before.' *September 2004*

Surviving a swarm of bullets

The blizzard of bullets lasted only seconds but to this day Geoffrey Van Rijssel is bewildered by the miracle of survival. A machine-gunner himself, he knew exactly what happened in what he calls 'a moment of inattention' in the front line at Arnhem. He stood up, presenting a brief target for a German machine-gun crew a few hundred yards away. Their MG42 could fire up to 1,400 bullets per minute.'I was looking up the road,' he recalls at his home in Bloxwich. 'Suddenly I was caught in this three or four-second burst. It was like a swarm. I felt I was enveloped by them. Somehow, I never got a scratch.' He later calculated that between sixty and ninety bullets buzzed around him, ripping his epaulettes, glancing off his steel helmet and wrecking the contents of his knapsack. A comrade ran to the same spot and was instantly killed. 'I warned him but he took the next burst of fire. He fell dead into my trench. A sergeant came across and asked: 'Everything under control then?' They were his last words. A sniper in the next building shot him dead. There was worse to come. In a deserted house at Oosterbeek, a stray bullet came through a closed door and ricocheted off a step. A sergeant screamed in agony, wounded deep in the groin. 'All we could do was inject him with our morphia, but we had to leave him. The Germans took good care of our blokes but we heard later that he had died of his wound in December.'

For Private Van Rijssel, born in Ghent to a Belgian father and an English mother, the story of Arnhem began in 1941 when he volunteered for the Army and was posted to the Royal Berkshire Regiment. Bored, he and thirty mates applied to join the Parachute Regiment. Only six were accepted. After para training the teenager, who spoke German, Dutch and French, was head-hunted by one of the most elite units of the British Army. The 21st Independent Parachute Company was composed largely of fluent linguists, including a smattering of German Jews who had fled Hitler's rule. Their job was to be first in at Arnhem, marking the landing grounds for the gliders and paratroops behind.

He recalls a perfect landing, marred by the freak death of a medic, struck in the head by a single bullet fired from a rifle which was accidentally dropped. The 186-strong company laid out their silk marker panels and, over the next two days, guided in the gliders and paratroops of the invasion force. Early in the operation the most serious danger was a massive wheel which came off a Horsa glider and hammered into the earth next to his slit trench. Years later he discovered the Horsa pilot was Alf 'Tug' Wilson who lived just up the road in Bloxwich. 'So I said, thanks very much.'

As the sleepless days and nights dragged on, the sense of failure spread. 'By the third day we should have been relieved. The Germans had Tiger tanks and we had nothing to combat them. I can still remember the sound of rusty tank tracks squeaking towards us.' Dog-tired, he was evacuated over the Rhine, struggled desperately up the steep bank and made it safely back to Nijmegen. He was back in Britain within days. He is fiercely proud to have fought at Arnhem and has been back several times. His sympathies are still with the Dutch. 'They thought we had liberated them. If only they had known.' As for his survival, Geoffrey Van Rijssel has no idea why he lived when so many good mates died. 'It was just luck, sheer luck. I'm afraid there was no credit at all on my part.' *September 2004*

Harassing the Nazis in Holland

Jim Klyn was a young member of the Dutch Resistance who witnessed the sacrifice of the Polish Brigade at Arnhem. He is covered with scars. Arrested and tortured by the Nazis, he suffered a cracked skull, broken nose and kicked ribs. In the advance towards Arnhem, revolver in hand, he came face to face with the sudden confusion and horror of war and collected more wounds. A solitary German SS soldier appeared before him and jabbed with his bayonet. The young Dutchman fell back, blood pouring from a hand wound. His revolver went off. The German dropped. Dead? 'I don't know. I don't want to know, ever. I thought I must have shot him but it was one of the Polish soldiers who had fired. My hand ached but it was just the recoil of my revolver.' In the same skirmish he took a shell splinter 'as hot as hell' in the leg (he still has the fragment) and a piece of mortar shrapnel in his neck.

Jim Klyn grew up in a small town near Eindhoven. In May 1940 Holland surrendered after a savage onslaught by the Nazis. He recalls the growing fury of life under German occupation. First a curfew was imposed. Then English textbooks were banned, making it impossible for him to study as an architect. Soon Dutch men were being rounded up for forced labour in Germany. Next the Dutch Jews were arrested and deported. 'I became a very angry young men,' he recalls.

In the early days the Dutch Resistance was a loose assortment of three-man cells, with secret signs and an armband inscribed 'Oranje' declaring their patriotism. 'We used to do harassment,' he recalls. 'It was little things like putting pebbles in railway points to jam them or letting off small explosions. It all tied up Germans troops. I remember once sitting quietly by the marshalling yards, making a note of the number of German tanks being moved. All this information was sent back to England.'

By 1943 Jim was a veteran guide on the 'Long Way', the route by which Dutch Jews, facing extermination by the Nazis, were smuggled across France into Switzerland. He also smuggled weapons dropped by the RAF to Resistance groups in Holland. Eventually he was arrested by the Germans and savagely interrogated. 'They shouted at me, "you want to kill Germans, don't you?" But I really didn't want to kill anyone. I just wanted to put them out of action.'Released after a beating, he slipped across the border to Belgium and was in Brussels on 3 September 1944 to see the Germans flee and the Canadians arrive. With liberation in the air, Jim Klyn tried to join the Dutch Army. But his weight had fallen to 6 stone and he was unfit to fight. Somehow he wangled accreditation as a reporter for the Dutch information ministry and grabbed a lift on the British armoured column heading north to relieve the soldiers at Arnhem. The mission failed and Arnhem turned into a bloodbath. One of the last acts was the landing of the Polish Brigade, which suffered heavy losses as it struggled to cross the Rhine to support the Brits. In the confusion of the dykeland, Jim Klyn and his posse of Poles saw high hopes turn to despair and recriminations. After the operation some tried to blame the Arnhem fiasco on the Poles and their fiery leader, General Stanislaw Sosabowski.

'The Poles were wonderful,' Jim says. 'The soldiers did the best they could. They were quiet men, very disciplined and well trained. Their logistics were good and their NCOs were the best, but the management was hopeless. General Sosabowski didn't speak much English but I heard him swearing in English all right. I will never forget that there are more Polish soldiers buried in Holland than Dutch soldiers.'

After the war he joined the RAF and trained briefly at Wolverhampton where he met his wife, Betty. They married in 1946 and she died in 1989. A retired computer consultant, Jim Klyn admits to occasional nightmares from his days in the resistance. But most of all he recalls his freedom, as a young, unmarried man with no ties, to fight back against Nazi oppression. 'I led a double life. I was free. I could do just what the hell I liked.' *September 2004*

Arnhem aftermath
Panic in the camp. Nazi guards began rounding up the British prisoners of war. Another death march was beginning. In the closing weeks of the Second World War in 1945 such scenes happened all over Germany. Captured servicemen were force-marched to camps further east, out of the hands of the advancing Allies. Those who fell by the wayside were

shot. Jack Hill from Willenhall, still nursing a serious bullet wound, took a huge and stomach-churning gamble. He and two comrades slipped into the camp latrines and hid, chest-deep in human excrement. It was a vile ordeal but it worked. A few hours later the advancing Americans arrived at the deserted camp. Jack Hill was free. He came home a hero, one of the men who won glory in the last great gamble of the war, Operation Market Garden.

Jack was a glider pilot on the ill-fated attempt to seize a string of bridges over the Rhine in Holland. He went into action on Sunday 17 September 1944. Before the epic flight he had a brief leave with his family in Willenhall. His younger brother Wilf recalls, 'We knew something was up. He told our sisters, "I'll bring you a present back from Holland," but that was all he could say.'With black humour, Jack Hill's massive Hamilcar glider was painted with the slogan 'The Undertaker and His Big Stiffs'. As he piloted the glider Jack chatted by telephone to a war correspondent from the *News Chronicle* in the towing aircraft. His account later featured in that newspaper and also in the popular *War Illustrated*.The confident mood quickly faded. The battle was all over in nine days, and the order was given to evacuate the last British pocket at the village of Oosterbeek.

Jack Hill was wounded and left behind. With a German bullet lodged close to his spine, he was patched up and taken into captivity. Back home in Willenhall, the family got the dreaded telegram 'Missing, presumed dead'. Jack's mother, Harriet, feared the worst but his father, Sam, a veteran of the First World War, was upbeat. 'My dad said Jack would turn up, like a bad penny. Maybe he was just trying to keep Mother's spirits up, but Jack did seem indestructible. You just felt he would turn up, somehow.'Two months later, a postcard in Italian arrived from the Red Cross. 'We didn't know what to do so we took it to the local Roman Catholic priest. He knew enough Italian to translate it and tell us that Jack was in a POW camp.'Months later the older brother Wilf hero-worshipped returned. It was a dramatic moment. 'I was in the old cinema in Willenhall,' he says. 'Suddenly they put this slide up on the screen saying Jack had come home.'

After the celebrations, a solemn chat. Jack Hill took his kid brother on one side. He told Wilf all about the savage fighting in Arnhem, the ordeal of POWs and the final horror of his hiding place in the cesspit. 'He knew I wanted to go in the Army and he wanted me to know about the reality of war.'Undeterred, Wilf went on to join the South Staffordshire Regiment, later transferring to the Cheshires. He saw action in the 1950s in Cyprus and Aden, rising to the rank of sergeant. His hero brother died of cancer. The memory is still sharp enough to bring tears to Wilf's eyes as we chat at his home in Great Wyrley. 'Jack was a great bloke. In everything he did, in his whole approach to life, he was a great guy.' *July 2004*

The explosion at Fauld . . .

It was 27 November 1944 and the morning was bright and clear. Workers on Upper Castle Hayes Farm watched as their bosses, Maurice Goodwin and his wife Mary, drove down the farm track towards the main road at Hanbury. It was the last thing they ever saw. There was the distant thud of a single detonation. And then the earth went mad as 100 feet below the farm an estimated 3,500 tons of bombs in an RAF store erupted. A slab of earth a quarter-mile across was torn to shreds and blasted half a mile into the sky, leaving a crater 300 feet deep. From the huge mushroom cloud that formed, massive chunks of rock, earth, trees and twisted metal fell back to earth.

By rights, twenty-one-year-old John Hardwick should have died. He was due to be feeding the cattle at one end of his father's farm. But after an early frost he was sent to cut roots for a neighbour with farm worker Fred Ford. 'It was a super, frosty, cloudless morning,' he recalls in his home near the church in Hanbury. 'Suddenly there was this almighty bang. We looked up and saw about 1½ acres of woodland going straight up in the air. We never saw it come down. Blast does funny things. They say it rocked houses in Rugby but I can't remember the earth moving. We ran to a hedge and got down flat.' He pauses, apologises. Somehow words are not enough to describe what he saw. 'This beautiful morning gave way to rain. Then the sky started to come down. We're talking about a sky full of soil.' The devastation was instantaneous and appalling. Seventy people, including farm workers, villagers and servicemen working in the RAF bomb store, known as 21 Maintenance Unit, were killed. Upper Castle Hayes Farm simply vanished. Two other farms were wrecked. Two hundred cattle perished, while a 30-foot dam on the hillside collapsed, pouring 6 million gallons of water in a torrent of mud and trees. The glutinous mass swept over the Goodwins' car and destroyed a nearby plasterboard factory, killing everyone inside. Half a mile away at Hanbury village, a roaring hot blast wrecked the village hall and the Cock Inn. At the village of Tutbury 3 miles away Vic Price rushed outside to see fully grown trees raining down like matchsticks and neighbours racing for cover. He had been working on a lathe in his garage; the shock wave, 'like some terrible nightmare', sheared it from its bolts. The blast damaged 150 buildings at Burton-on-Trent 6 miles away. It shook houses all across the Midlands, was heard as far away as Weston-super-Mare and was picked up on seismographs in Switzerland. As the villagers emerged from cover, half-blinded by dirt and mud, they looked out on something resembling a First World War battlefield. Hills, woods and ancient streams had been swept away. The whole area was pockmarked with craters caused by falling debris. There was no electricity, water or telephones. John Hardwick made his way through Hanbury. Not a chimney pot remained. A neighbour's house was no more than a heap of bricks. The village hall had been blasted into the next field, 'with piano keys all over the place. The crater looked like a wide ice-cream cornet. It was a moonscape, with trees upended, nothing living or growing.'Near the crater rim John came across an air shaft from the gypsum mine. A miner, Bill Watson, staggered out, telling of bodies at the bottom of the shaft. 'He hadn't the faintest idea which way to start walking home. You see, all the contours had changed. There were no landmarks.'The shell-shocked survivors had witnessed the biggest detonation of conventional explosives in either world war. In an instant Fauld had been destroyed by six times as much high explosive as the Germans dropped during the infamous Coventry blitz. The explosion at Fauld was the biggest in Britain, and was eclipsed only by the nuclear bombs dropped on the Japanese towns of Hiroshima and Nagasaki the following year.

But what had gone wrong? No-one will ever know for sure. All those at the heart of the bomb store were killed. There were wild rumours of an American 'super-bomb' and of three planes seen diving near the site before the explosion. There was talk of sabotage, either by spies, escaped German prisoners of war or by former Italian soldiers employed in the store. There was even a theory that the IRA were involved. But the likeliest explanation is that the disaster at Fauld was a ghastly accident caused by inexperienced staff taking short-cuts. Yet Whitehall kept the findings of the board of inquiry secret for thirty years, an act of petty secrecy that merely added to the conspiracy theories.

The story began in 1941 when the RAF needed somewhere to store thousands of bombs. The disused gypsum mines at Fauld seemed ideal. As the air war over Germany intensified, RAF Fauld was receiving and distributing 20,000 tons of bombs per month. Soon the 18 officers, 475 other ranks and 445 civilians at the base could not cope with the workload. The problem was solved by offering jobs to 195 Italian prisoners of war from the nearby Hilton POW camp. Few were experienced in handling explosives. On the day of the disaster the jobs to be done included an inspection of three 1,000-lb bombs that had been damaged in service and returned to Fauld for repair. It was a dangerous, highly skilled job. Yet an armourer who survived the blast told the board of inquiry that he saw one of his colleagues using a brass chisel to dismantle one of the bombs – a practice strictly forbidden. This could have detonated the bomb: the first explosion heard by witnesses before the rest of the 3,500-ton store erupted. The rescue attempt was heroic but hopeless. Firemen were beaten back by poison gas, which killed one rescuer and five miners in the nearby gypsum mine. The bomb store was closed and it took a year of hard, hazardous work to recover the last of the unexploded bombs. Bodies were found for up to eighteen months afterwards. John Hardwick, who became clerk to the parish council, remembers the village bobby reverentially walking every day in front of the heavy recovery machines to make sure no corpses were mangled. He recalls the school turned into a morgue, the school caretaker washing her husband's body, one of the first to be recovered. He tells how the village embraced its orphans. 'There was a fund that made sure they weren't financially deprived, and the village made sure they didn't suffer social deprivation. We were a very close village.'The village hall, the pub and the rest of the damaged buildings were rebuilt or repaired. The crater's jagged edges became mellowed with grass, ferns and conifers. *November 1994*

...and an explanation?

It was as close to hell as Malcolm Kidd ever hopes to get. There was a blast of hot air through the old mine tunnel at Fauld, followed by a blast of cold. Then everything went black. At the mouth of the old gypsum cave, commandeered four years earlier as an RAF bomb store, he found a scene from Hades.'I will never forget it,' he recalls at his home in Wilmslow, Cheshire. 'The shock had set off boxes of incendiary bombs and they were blazing away. We found the body of a policeman. Half his head had been blown away. Then we nearly got shot by the RAF Regiment. The explosion had sent the cattle and sheep crazy. The soldiers were trying to shoot them, and didn't realise you had to hit a cow in the head to kill it.' Malcolm Kidd and his mates had survived the biggest high-explosive detonation of either world war. Young aircraftman Kidd attended the court of inquiry as a witness, but, for reasons he has never understood, was not called. The inquiry concluded that the explosion was probably caused by an accident, but Malcolm Kidd tells a different story.

On the morning of the explosion, 27 November 1944, he was sent to deal with two 1,000-pound bombs which had been recovered from a crashed RAF bomber. The routine was simple. Ordered by a sergeant, Malcolm Kidd stencilled each bomb with 'For Dumping in Deep Water'. They were then to be jettisoned at sea. But soon afterwards a civilian munitions worker intervened. 'There were RAF and civilians working at Fauld. The RAF were fully trained and did things by the book. But the civilians were a law unto themselves. While I was in the restroom a civilian said, "I'll get some Stillsons [large wrenches], take the noses off those crash bombs, and we can send them out again." It was a make-do-and-mend mentality.'

91

In any case, he recalls, short-cuts with safety were part of daily life at RAF Fauld. 'There were hairy things going on all the time, but there was a war on.' Malcolm is convinced that the civilian caused the explosion by trying to unscrew the nose-pistol on one of the 1,000lb bombs. To this day he regrets not intervening. 'But I was very young and very junior. My father had been in the Guards and I was taught to carry out orders and not to question anything. I was just an ordinary aircraftman. It wasn't my job to say don't do that. This is the true story. I want to put the record straight.' *December 1994*

The Tommy they couldn't cook

The Brits called it the Ronson. The Germans called it the Tommy Cooker. Both were referring to the Sherman tank, a robust and reliable fighting machine with one deadly flaw. When hit by enemy shells the American-built Sherman had a terrifying tendency to burst into flames. They called it 'brewing up'. Sixty years on old tankies still remember the screams of their doomed mates trapped in stricken Shermans. Albert Fleet was dead lucky, for his Sherman was hit not once but twice by the most feared gun in the Nazi armoury. He was riddled with shrapnel but lived to tell the tale. The first time he was saved by a million-to-one chance. The second time the Sherman started to 'brew up', but inexplicably the fire went out. Albert Fleet is the Tommy they couldn't cook.

As he talks in the cosy history centre at his home village of Pelsall near Walsall, the years fall away. It is December 1944. The Brummie lad is a Sherman gunner with the Fife & Forfar Yeomanry and his tank is nudging forward up a 'beautiful straight road' in Holland. 'I thought we might get a few miles without any trouble but after a few hundred yards, bang! The two tanks in front went up in flames. I turned the turret to the left and then all of a sudden, bang! The commander asked why I had fired the gun but I knew I hadn't.'

By the next morning's light the mystery was solved. A shell from an 88mm gun, the Germans' most powerful anti-tank weapon, had struck the Sherman on a plate by the gun barrel base. The impact had set off the Sherman's gun and the recoil miraculously soaked up the energy of the shell. 'It worked like a shock-absorber. One inch either side and the shell would have gone straight through the turret and killed us all.'

There was worse to come. At Christmas 1944 the Germans launched their last great offensive, the Battle of the Bulge, smashing through American lines in the Ardennes forest. A small British force, including the Fife & Forfar Yeomanry, was thrown into a counter-attack. Albert Fleet recalls how the British tanks caught German troops in the open and killed dozens with their machine-guns. 'It was a pity. They were probably good lads, just like we were.'

On 4 January 1945 his luck ran out. A German Tiger tank got the Sherman in its sights. An 88mm shell struck with a massive impact. He recalls a confusion of light, darkness, flashes, noise, silence and the scramble as his three crewmates got out. His legs were paralysed with shrapnel wounds. Unable to move, he watched the flames and, bizarrely, worried about losing his beret. 'And then the flames died down. I got on the radio and said, get me out. Someone said hang on. Well, what else was I going to do?' After more than half an hour in the smoking Sherman he was pulled to safety and on his way back home. 'I'm a lucky man. A very, very lucky man.' *December 2004*

VE Day – Victory in Europe

VE Day for Joe Gough came deep inside Germany, at Luneberg Heath. The British were on one side of the river, their Russian allies on the other. In the early hours of 7 May 1945 the teleprinter suddenly clattered and Joe, a Royal Corps of Signals message handler, stared in wonder as the most important print-out of the war arrived. It was from General Eisenhower at the Allies' supreme headquarters, for distribution to all army units. The words that millions of servicemen had waited six years to hear had arrived: 'Effective immediately. Offensive operations Allied Expeditionary Force will cease.'

'Being a signaller, I saw the signal before anyone else,' recalls Joe at his home in Wolverhampton. 'We had an idea that something was coming but we didn't know when.' The relief was intense. His unit had been fighting towards Berlin ever since D-Day+3, eleven months earlier.

When peace came in May 1945 British soldiers were in every corner of the world. But none had a stranger job than Lieutenant Ken Jackson, of Kidderminster, late of the 71st King's African Rifles, who was in Somalia. After service in Burma his battalion returned to British Somaliland to be disbanded, leaving the young officer facing the boring prospect of barrack life in Nairobi. 'So instead I volunteered to serve with the Somalia Gendarmerie, an Army-controlled glorified band of units keeping order and holding at bay the local brigands.' VE Day found him with his fellow officer Gerry Stagg, of Great Barr, who later became his best man, on a remote hill in the Ogaden, hundreds of miles from the nearest city. 'Our radio was broken, so there was little contact with the outside world. During this time peace came to Europe. When we heard, via a message from HQ, all I thought was that now, maybe, they would supply our troops in Burma properly for a change.' For Ron Wood and his comrades on tank transporters, VE Day came early. The Royal Army Service Corps unit had followed the fighting from D-Day across France and into Germany and witnessed the last major offensive by Hitler's once-dreaded Luftwaffe. 'A heavy formation of jets attacked the area,' he recalls at his Wolverhampton home. 'It seemed that every gun around us put up a terrific fire and five or six were shot down.' His unit, 451 Tank Transporter Company, moved on towards Hamburg. 'It was very slow moving because of vast numbers of Germans surrendering all along our route. Finally, on about May 4, we stopped. We knew it was near the end. A dispatch rider passed us, waving. Then our sergeant came out with a bottle of schnapps and said, "It's all over, lads." We were totally exhausted and all fell asleep, at last.'For Cyril Wilde of Bilston, and for thousands of fellow Brits, VE Day meant the end of captivity as a prisoner of war. The young para had been taken prisoner at Arnhem in 1944 after a career that had taken him to battles in Africa, Italy and Sicily. Three months after Arnhem he found himself in a working party near the German city of Liepzig, 'repairing the railway lines and dodging the RAF as they came down strafing us'.

Other POWs, robbed of their watches, lost track of time, but Mr Wilde kept a note of each passing day on the back of a photograph of his wife. 'The day of liberation came. The German guards left us and we were on our own. Then came the Russians. They told us the Yanks were on the other side of the Elbe and two days later we contacted them. The Yanks gave us chocolate and cigarettes. Then we had a good long leave.'For John Denis Potts, the D-Day glider pilot incarcerated in a German POW camp, VE Day brought blessed relief and the grisly opportunity to witness an execution. As the end of the war approached he and his 20,000 fellow Allied airmen in Luckenwalde camp had orders to stay put. But with RAF bombing intensifying and the Russian Army closing in, the POWs felt like sitting ducks, liable to be hit at any time. 'So every night, during darkness and with RAF Bomber Command keeping all heads down, it was a simple operation to cut through the adjoining compounds and into the safety of the Russian Army.'

Together with the Russians, John Potts and his comrades foraged for food as hunger and typhus stalked the camp. Shortly before VE Day the Russians relieved the camp, crushing the perimeter wire with their tanks. Mr Potts recalls 8 May 1945. It was warm and sunny and the Russians were suddenly celebrating. 'The small streets near the sidings were filled with soldiers. The singing, dancing, bread, sausage, cheese and the non-labelled bottles of white spirit told us all we needed to know – the war was over.'

Soviet officers showed the RAF men around their tanks and took them to the local police station where two Russian deserters, drunk and 'in a sickening condition', were awaiting the firing squad, having been caught looting and raping. 'We were invited to their execution scheduled for the following morning. We declined on the grounds of a previous engagement.'For sailors John Price and Edwin Garner peace in Europe coincided with hell on the high seas. They were shipmates on the aircraft carrier HMS *Formidable*, off Okinawa, on VE Day. It was suddenly attacked by Japanese kamikaze suicide bombers, one of which crashed on the flight deck. 'I was on the forward gun turret,' recalls Edwin. 'We couldn't see what happened but we felt the impact, like a great shuddering.'Folk back home were celebrating victory, but the sailors in the Far East were patching up their ships and preparing for the next onslaught. But three months later they witnessed a memorable sight. One morning in August 1945 the crew of HMS *Formidable* looked up and saw a small formation of American warplanes. One of them was the Superfortress Enola Gay, carrying the first atom bomb to Hiroshima. A few days later, with Hiroshima and Nagasaki both destroyed by A-bombs, the Japanese surrendered. John Price remembers HMS *Formidable* steaming into Sydney Harbour in triumph, leading the victory fleet. 'Later we all joined in a victory parade through the streets of Sydney. What a great joy. I wish it could be shown again on television so that people could see what a grand time we had. There were men from *Formidable*, *Implacable*, *Victorious*, *Black Prince* and *Grenville*, with the band of the Marines.'For Reuben Welsh and his comrades in the Sherman tanks of the Staffordshire Yeomanry, VE Day dawned on the banks of the Elbe. Deep inside the shattered Third Reich, the troopers were veterans of the D-Day landings and the bloody Normandy campaign. They had fought half-way across Europe. By the time the war ended British tank crews were among the most professional and experienced soldiers anywhere. VE Day was greeted with mixed feelings.

'For us, the end of the war was an anti-climax. We had been so used to being in action for so many years that, when the end came, we felt somewhat lost. However, this did not last long. We re-crossed the Elbe to a small village not far from Belsen concentration camp. Here we experienced what the end of the war really meant. Everyone knew that at that moment they were alive, that they were not going to lose their lives. Germany at that time was full of people moving. They were going home. Interspersed with the civilians were German soldiers. They all looked the same, tired, dusty, with three or four days' growth of beard. Even the poor people of Belsen in their striped pyjama-type suits could be seen trying to walk home. After years of suffering the urge was so great.'

If VE Day seemed a long time a-coming, so did little Marjorie May Corns. She was two weeks overdue when her mother, Emily, went into labour on VE Day. Marjorie arrived at the family home in High Street, Wombourne, just as the church bells opposite were ringing out for victory. During the war years church bells had been silenced, to be sounded only as a warning of invasion. 'It was a wonderful day,' recalls Mrs Corns, living in Wombourne close to her daughter, now Mrs

Marjorie Sutton. 'At three o'clock Mr Churchill began his speech announcing the end of the war. I started in labour and she was born just as the victory bells rang out. We hadn't heard our bells.' So why wasn't a child born on this special day given a more appropriate name? 'Yes, she might have been called Victoria,' says her mother, 'but I had promised to name her after Marjorie, her godmother. But we gave her the middle name of May to remember the month.' Connie Wall was a twenty-one-year-old serving in what she calls 'a very exclusive unit', the Women's Timber Corps. An offshoot of the Land Army, the corps felled and sawed timber for the war effort, producing everything from sawdust to coffin boards. Connie and her 'Lumber Jill' colleagues were sent to work at a timber yard in Stafford, shifting heavy baulks of timber and helping with the sawing and loading. 'We grumbled like mad but in fact we all loved it, especially the outdoor work, and we built up some beautiful muscles. On VE Day I was driving a mobile crane, stacking timber on a lorry. When the announcement came, everyone downed tools and went absolutely wild. The management decided the best thing to do was to give everyone the rest of the day off. So we all went straight down the nearest pub. It was a memorable day.'

For Margaret Simmons and her family from the Nazi-occupied Channel Islands, VE Day meant the end of disruption, fear and misery as prisoners. Most of the islanders endured occupation as best they could, but because Margaret's father was English, he and his wife and four children, along with scores of other families were deported to Germany. After a nightmarish journey by cargo ship and railway wagons, the family was interned for three years in two camps deep inside Hitler's Third Reich. Margaret, who now lives in Wednesfield, was aged seven when they were deported. She recalls: 'The memories are so vivid. I remember my sister reaching through a gap in the camp wire and finding a hen's egg. My mother made us all egg sandwiches that day. It was called a prisoner of war camp but it was for civilians and we were not treated too badly. Of course, we children could not understand how bad it was for our parents, being away from Jersey. The second camp was in a huge monastery. Opposite, there was a big stone building and my father said that, when the war was over, men would go rushing into that building. That's exactly what happened. One day the American soldiers came and suddenly the two big gates at the back of the camp were thrown open. We kids just ran out. We went mad. Our parents had no idea where we were. I remember the streets were full of tanks going by. The soldiers said they didn't even know our camp was there.'

After the war the family settled in England. By now they were six-strong: Margaret's younger brother, Bruce, was born in the prison-camp hospital.For Fred Knowles, VE Day came as the 53rd Welsh Division drove into the bomb-shattered German city of Hamburg. A thirty-year-old private with the divisional HQ, he witnessed tens of thousands of beaten, demoralised Germans surrendering. 'The streets were full of them. You could hardly see the British guards at all. There was about one Tommy to every hundred Germans. The Germans just wanted to give up and go home,' he recalls at his home in Bentley. 'Hamburg was in ruins, totally ruined. I never thought they could ever rebuild it but I'm told it's beautiful today. VE Day was a wonderful day for us. We were in this hotel, drinking Schnapps and watching the prisoners. To be honest, we were all a bit tipsy.'Private Knowles ended his war in a moment of supreme irony. Before he joined up he worked at a munitions factory in West Bromwich and once heard the infamous Lord Haw-Haw, William Joyce, broadcast a Nazi threat to bomb the factory. A few violent years later Fred Knowles and his comrades set up their divisional headquarters in the very hotel in Hamburg from which Joyce, who was later hanged for treason, had broadcast. 'Our general strung a line of lights up the side of the hotel with a huge W for Wales. You could see it all over Hamburg.'

For Fred Taylor of Bilston, VE Day came after some of the hardest fighting of the war. A para with the legendary 6th Airborne Division, he had taken part in the airborne assault on the Rhine on 24 March, 'just in time for morning coffee', as he recalls. It was the biggest airborne operation of the war and it was followed by a hotly contested drive deep into Germany. But as the Russians advanced from the east, resistance weakened and the roads filled with German refugees and soldiers. 'I remember an NCO came to our headquarters to say there were some high-ranking German officers outside. They were in long black leather coats. One of them explained that their armoured brigade had never been defeated in battle and they wished to surrender with honour, bearing arms. Our company commander was very polite but told them there were no terms. The surrender was unconditional.' Fred recalls German villages with white sheets hanging from every window in surrender. He remembers, too, that his own outlook was bleak, for the paras were to be used in a mass air assault to recapture Singapore from the Japanese. 'Word got around that we had been written off before we had even been sent.' Before the plan was put into operation the atom bombs were dropped on Japan, and the war was over.

VE Day came and went for Eric Shaw and his pals serving with the 'forgotten' 14th Army in the Far East, grinding down Japanese resistance in the last bloody stages of the Burma campaign. He and his mates in the Royal Air Force Regiment, experts in defending airfields, had been hastily re-trained as foot soldiers to plug the gaps in the British infantry divisions. If the Japanese had known their opponents were so short of trained soldiers, says Eric of Parkfields, Wolverhampton, they might have made one last desperate push for India. As it was, he and his comrades spent VE Day on the offensive, fighting towards Rangoon. 'We were aware that many thousands of people were celebrating and having a knees-up in London, without very much thought of what was going on in other parts of the world.' The Forgotten Army was resigned to fighting all the way to Tokyo. It was three months later that the war in the Far East was suddenly ended by a new and terrible weapon. 'If it hadn't been for the atom bombs on Hiroshima and Nagasaki I reckon we'd still be out there.' *May 1995*

VJ Day

The sights Ron Walker of Tipton saw as a prisoner of the Japanese are forever branded in his memory. 'We were on the boat towards Java. All the sick were lying on the deck and one airman had been caught stealing fish from the galley. He was set upon by six guards. They beat him senseless. Then this sergeant-major came with his sword. We were forced to watch. The sergeant-major chopped his head off with the sword. The head and the body were just thrown over the side.'

Ron Walker was in the RAF when war broke out and was shipped out to the Far East in 1941, serving with a squadron of Hurricane fighters. But the RAF machines were outclassed and outnumbered by the Japanese Zero fighters. Some pilots flew to safety in India. On 8 March 1942 Leading Aircraftsman Walker, aged just twenty-three, was one of thousands of Allied servicemen taken prisoner. In the three years that followed a third of the POWs in his group died of starvation, disease, ill-treatment or by casual execution. Three pilots caught trying to escape from the prisoner of war pen were executed by beheading. His group were put to work on the Indonesian isle of Ambon, building an airfield despite constant bombing. The work was backbreaking but any shirking was dealt with by a brutal beating. 'The ships couldn't come in to harbour so we were taken a mile out to sea to push these 45 gallon drums of diesel to the shore. 'You just had to live each day at a time. If you got through a day without a beating it was a good day – and there were very few of those.' By August 1945 Ron Walker and his weary, skeletal mates were back at the infamous Changi Jail, building foxholes and defence ditches. But they were never needed. News came, via hidden radio sets, that the Japanese had surrendered. 'One day the Japs disappeared and the Red Caps [British military police] took over. It was as quick as that. I'd come out to the Far East weighing 10 stone 11 pounds. When we were liberated I was 5 stone 10 pounds. I never expected to survive. If anyone had told me in 1945 that I'd still be around sixty years later I would never have believed them. It's time to forgive, but I can never forget what the Japanese did to us. People in this country had no idea what was going on.' *August 2005*

Hope in a tropical sky

In the bleakest depths of despair, John Pratt of Sedgley raised his eyes to the skies and found hope. He was a prisoner of war of the Japanese, a young British Army signaller caught in the collapse of Singapore in February 1942. The surrender of the 130,000 British garrison to a Japanese force of just 30,000 was the darkest moment in the Second World War. 'I never wear the medals. I was disgusted with the whole thing. It was so unnecessary.'

Marched off into captivity, he was held first in the notorious Changi Jail complex and then used as forced labour, building embankments and bridges. 'Some days all hope deserted you and you just wanted to die. I remember one night looking up into this immense tropical sky. The whole heavens were alive with planets and stars and somehow it restored some sort of faith to me. It made me think things weren't as desperate as they seemed to me.'As the end of the war approached his unit was moved, first back to Singapore and then to Saigon. On the voyage the POWs were herded below decks into a stinking, airless hold. To their terror the big convoy was attacked during the night, probably by American submarines. 'The sound of ships breaking up could be clearly heard through the water. We were battened down and you can imagine our feelings. The next morning we were allowed on deck in small groups. We could see that all that remained of the convoy was one destroyer and ourselves.'He relishes the memory of a camp parade soon afterwards. 'We were herded on to an airstrip to be viewed as spoils of war by a visiting Japanese dignitary. Japanese troops were formed up as a guard of honour for his plane to land.' But the plane that appeared at the end of the camp was not a Japanese transport: it was a formidable Lightning fighter-bomber from a United States aircraft carrier. As the Japanese scattered the Brits cheered. 'We all applauded, and then we got beaten round the ears by the Japs,' he recalls.But a few days later the war was over, and the emaciated POWs were flown to Rangoon to be shipped home. For many the transition from imprisonment to liberty was a testing time. 'My memory was shot to pieces. After being fettered for so long, all I wanted to do was to roam around the country and visit some of the places I had been based.'He married and studied engineering at London University. In his career as a bridge-builder and metallurgist, he survived three falls. Any of the falls could have proved fatal. Each escape reinforced the hope he first experienced under a tropical sky in captivity all those years ago: 'I seem to have a charmed life.' *August 2005*

The day the Japs saluted us

For Ken Hill, VJ Day came in the notorious Changi Jail near Singapore. 'We knew something was happening because some of our officers had hidden radios,' he recalls at his home in Swindon near Wolverhampton. 'They told us not to do anything out of the ordinary because the Americans had just dropped an atom bomb on Japan. Then we heard another bomb had been dropped. The next morning we went out and, instead of us saluting the Japs, they saluted us.'

For the twenty-four-year-old corporal mechanic, it was the end of three-and-a-half bestial years as a prisoner of war. After the fall of Singapore he was part of a huge working party marched up the jungle to work on the infamous Burma Railway. 'Seven thousand of us started out. Within six months four thousand of them were dead. I doubt if more then a thousand survived the war.' From the outset the Japanese were eager to show off their ruthlessness. He recalls his captors gleefully showing off severed heads of Singapore civilians, stuck on spikes in the city to terrorise the population. Back home in Netherton his parents, Ernie and Elsie, were suffering untold anguish. They had three sons in uniform, and had barely received notice that Ken and his older brother Geoff had been taken by the Japanese when news came through that their other lad, Granville, was missing after the German invasion of Crete. Thankfully Granville was merely separated briefly from his RAF unit. 'It wasn't until I was a parent myself that I realised what my mother must have gone through. I honestly don't know how she survived.'

Ken managed to meet Geoff in Changi but his brother was soon shipped out to a prison camp in Borneo. It was a poignant parting. His eyes sparkle with emotion. 'I can picture it now as the lorry came past, and they all shouted "cheerio!" as they went.'

On the Burma Railway, where it was reckoned one Allied POW died for every sleeper laid, the Brits coped as best they could. 'I think I survived because I was big and fit to begin with. I never blamed anyone. I was a Territorial before the war and I always took the view that no-one ever pressed me to join the Army. What happened to me was my own fault. I didn't hate anyone. It was a big experience and you just had to get on with it. After we were liberated some of the Australians went round, finding the Japs who were the worst so that they could be tried and hanged. But we just wanted to get home.' From the fall of Singapore in February 1942 until liberation in August 1945 Ken had eaten nothing but rice. On weekdays we ate our first meal in the dark and just ate it straight down. But on Sundays we got it in the light. We could see what we were actually eating. It took ages, picking it all out.' Like many survivors, Ken Hill knows that the stuff he ate in the dark, a sickening blend of beetles and maggots, probably helped keep him alive. When it was all over he had a chance meeting with the pilot of Bill Slim, the legendary commander of the 'Forgotten' 14th Army. The ex-POW was able to scribble a reassuring note to his mother and slip it on the general's plane. She got the good news within a few days. Getting home took a little longer. 'We came home by slow boat. Would you believe, the first meal they gave us was rice. There was a riot, but the captain explained if they gave us meat or anything rich it could kill us. But I have never eaten rice since. I had my share in the war, thanks.' Ken's brother Geoff survived as a Japanese POW. It was not until the end of 1945 that the three sons were reunited with their family in Netherton. At first Ken suffered many nightmares, but now he thinks he is over them. Brenda, his wife is not so sure. 'Sometimes he will shout in the night,' she says, 'and I think he must be dreaming about it.' Ken Hill believes, as so many old POWs believe, that he owes his life to the atom bomb. It is widely believed that if the Allies had landed on mainland Japan all POWs would have been slaughtered. 'If they hadn't dropped the atom bombs I wouldn't be here today.' *August 2005*

THE POST-WAR YEARS

Bloody Partition in India

Out of a clear Indian night the troop train was suddenly raked with rifle and machine-gun fire. One of two young officers sitting opposite Tony Hearne fell dead. A gunman appeared at the window with a shotgun and fired, point-blank. 'It took the head off the other officer,' Tony recalls. 'There was blood all over the compartment. It was dripping from the roof.' The killer bobbed down to re-load his shotgun. A few seconds later he appeared again at the window and aimed his weapon at a wounded soldier. But by then Tony Hearne was ready. 'I remembered something my father had told me. Never point a gun at someone unless you intend to kill them. I shot him – bang! – and his face disappeared. His gun went off, but it just blew a hole in the ceiling.'

This was India in 1947 as the British moved out and Muslims and Hindus set about slaughtering each other in the horrors that gave birth to Partition and the new state of Pakistan. Tony Hearne talks quietly in a clipped, crystal-clear voice. Here, at home in Wombourne, is the authentic voice of British rule, the so-called Raj that governed India for 300 years. He has not seen his beloved India since 1948 and yet his accent is untouched by time. His Ts are pronounced as Ds in the Indian fashion. Close your eyes and it could be the BBC's veteran India reporter, Mark Tulley. This, he says, is how you talk when you have spent a lifetime explaining things in great detail to workers across half the planet. Tony was a child of the British Raj, a son of Gerald Frederick Hearne, colonial civil servant and magistrate in Lahore. The magistrate's many duties included stamping out the practice of suttee, Hindu widows throwing themselves on their husband's funeral pyre. Educated at the famous St George's College in the Himalayas, young Tony served in the Ordnance Corps during the Second World War, supplying the British Army in Burma with thousands of tons of everything from bullets to beans. He rose to become Conductor of Ordnance, the most senior NCO in the British Army.

When the war ended in 1945 India's demand for independence from Britain could no longer be denied. But the speed of the British withdrawal took many by surprise. 'Everyone thought it would continue in the same old colonial way. There was no real desire to go home to England. People wanted to retire to gorgeous places like Darjeeling and live like kings on their pensions.' The reality was the sudden collapse of law and order and ethnic slaughter. 'It seemed impossible that this wonderful lifestyle, unequalled in any other colony of the Empire, would within a few short years be shattered after a horrific sectarian blood bath, also unequalled in the history of the Empire. You know, I have killed, quite deliberately killed, a number of my fellow men.'

There is no hint of regret or bravado in the old man's words. In August 1947, on a troop train headed from Calcutta to Lahore, Tony Hearne became the only European to witness a massacre which, he believes, was orchestrated by the Indian Army in revenge for an earlier atrocity by Muslims. As the train, packed with Muslim solders, prepared to leave the station, he saw British and Indian officers in a furious argument. The Indians won. The Muslims were forced to hand over their weapons before the journey began. A few hours later there was a banging and shouting. The last four carriages, carrying the British officers, were detached from the train. 'It was all set up. They wanted to avoid an international affair, so they stopped all the British officers being witnesses. When the shooting started it was the Indian Army, no more than 300 yards from the train.' After killing the man with the shotgun, Tony grabbed the wounded officer and made his way from the bloodsoaked train to a station. The platform was covered with Muslim dead, victims of another killing frenzy. By the time the agony of Partition was over an estimated 12 million Indians were homeless and up to a million dead. *January 2008*

Under fire in Korea

For teenage conscripts like Hadley Harris of Kidderminster serving with the Middlesex Regiment, the Korean crisis came at the end of a plum, year-long posting to Hong Kong. 'We were called together by the colonel and he said, "Men, you have been chosen to represent the United Nations." We hadn't a clue what was going on but I didn't want to miss it. The trouble was, you had to be nineteen to go into the front line and I was still only eighteen.'

The Americans were first into the fray. The North Korean invasion began in June 1950 and the Yanks had been in action since 5 July, when they suffered a mauling as Communist tanks overran their positions. 'When are we going to see some of those Aussies and Brits up here?' one hard-pressed US squaddie demanded in the world's media. On 26 July Britain decided to send troops to the Americans' aid. On 29 August the Middlesex Regiment and the Argyll & Sutherland Highlanders made an unopposed landing, to the skirl of a pipe band, from the aircraft carrier *Unicorn* on Korea's south-east coast. Ringing in their ears was the gung-ho farewell message of the Far East Commander-in-Chief, Lieutenant-General Sir John Harding: 'Shoot quickly, shoot straight and shoot to kill.'Hadley Harris was there. It was his nineteenth birthday, and any hopes of a great adventure quickly faded. Korea was a dirty, killing war. 'I don't like to tell war stories because it exalts war,' says the London-born retired engineer at his Kidderminster home. 'War is the worst thing that anyone can get involved in.'The Brits' first battle began with a lecture on the need to assault Plum Pudding Hill, held by the Communists. 'Look here, you chaps,' said a Middlesex officer in best staff-college tones. 'Those people up there have no right to be there and we're jolly well going to push them off that blooming hill.'

But the Brits advanced into a mortar ambush. A quick-thinking lieutenant saved the day by coolly calling down artillery fire, winning the Military Cross in the process. But as his pals fell dead and terribly wounded, Hadley Harris understood the reality of war. Later he was on the winning side as the American-led forces caught the Communists unawares with the surprise amphibious landings at Inchon.

By the end of 1950 the UN forces were at the Chinese border and Red China suddenly entered the war, sending human waves of troops. The UN retreated and the Korean War settled into three bloody seesaw years of attacks and counter-attacks. By the time the war ended in July 1953, with a ceasefire that is still in effect today, an estimated 2½ million men, women and children were dead. Most were civilians and, for all the horrors he saw in battle, it is their suffering that Hadley Harris, who served in Korea for a year, remembers most keenly. 'We saw thousands upon thousands of these poor people, with all their little children, running up and down the roads, not knowing where to go or what to do. It was terrible to see such suffering. In a famine everyone wants to help, but in that war there was nothing that could be done to help. It's awful to think about.' *February 1990*

The Glorious Glosters
The moment he opens the door you understand the nickname. Lofty Large is one very big man. For sixteen years, on behalf of you and me,

this 6 foot 6 inch character with a chest like a beer barrel did one of the dirtiest jobs the nation has to offer.

Lofty Large served with the SAS. Today he is one of the few ex-SAS men to talk about the 'various odd places around the world' where he and his comrades in the Special Air Service Regiment put their special talents to work. 'They used us when they wanted a scalpel instead of a meat cleaver,' says Lofty Large over a coffee in the lounge of his comfortable home a few hundred yards from the barracks of 22 SAS Regiment in Hereford. Like many former SAS troopers he has settled in the town. His first book, *One Man's SAS*, has become required reading for students of the regiment. His second book relates his experiences as an ordinary soldier in Korea. *One Man's Korea* is a fine tribute to the 'Glorious Glosters', the Gloucestershire Regiment whose proudest moment was the epic defence at the Imjin river in April 1951. For nearly four days fewer than a thousand British soldiers held off twenty-seven thousand Chinese troops until, overwhelmed by firepower and sheer numbers, the Glosters ceased to exist as a fighting unit.

Badly wounded, Lofty Large was one of hundreds of Glosters taken prisoner and confined in a Chinese POW camp for two years. He survived, he insists, on little more than a burning confidence in cause, country and comrades. 'I spent two years in the greatest political university in the world. But the indoctrination didn't work because I had faith in everything that was British – the country, the Army, the unit and myself. Korea was a job that had to be done to stop the spread of Communism. I don't regret volunteering for it, and being a prisoner stood me in good stead. I knew afterwards that I could cope with the worst that could happen.'

After repatriation Lofty Large volunteered again, this time for the SAS, and served in a series of undercover campaigns, from Aden and Borneo to Malaya and Oman. He saw nothing to change his view that the British soldier, the 'Trog', is the best in the world. Sadly, he says, echoing the views of so many old soldiers, successive governments have failed to match the commitment of their fighting men. 'They could send thousands of young men who had done nothing wrong 8,000 miles to the Falklands, to die a horrible, screaming death on the battlefield – but they haven't got the guts to hang a granny-killer. It doesn't make sense. I've seen my friends killed on battlefields. They didn't do anything wrong: they were just carrying out the policies of their government. But that same government hasn't the guts to hang someone who is really evil, so we spend thousands keeping these bums behind bars. Politicians ought to read Kipling's poem *If*. That's what politicians have lost – the common touch. They're out of touch with the people. Everything has become so defensive. We'll get to the stage where, rather than shoot a mad dog in the street, they'll issue everyone with a suit of armour. There are so many idiots in this country. But someone has to be the cutting edge of government policy. Someone has to do it.'

Lofty Large wielded the scalpel. And no, he has no regrets. *February 1989*

Suez

In 1956 the Suez Canal, passing through Egypt, was operated by Britain and France, who shared its massive profits. For Egypt, still smarting from the 1948 creation of the state of Israel, the canal was a festering irritation. On 26 July 1956 the Egyptian president, Colonel Gamal Abdel Nasser, nationalised the Suez Canal. Britain and France secretly plotted with Israel – a deal denied for years afterwards. Under the joint plan Israel would invade Egypt; Britain and France would then intervene, allegedly to keep the warring sides apart. In reality the Anglo-French force would re-take the Suez Canal. All through the summer thousands of British reservists who thought their army days were over were recalled. At camps in Britain and Cyprus they prepared for a massive show of force. On 29 October 1956 Israeli troops invaded Egypt's Sinai Peninsula. Two days later British and French military forces attacked and invaded Egypt's canal zone after President Nasser had refused their offer of creating a buffer zone between Israel and Egypt.

And then the new world order asserted itself. Britain and France, both convinced their cause was just, found themselves regarded as bullies for attacking a weak nation. The real post-war superpowers got involved. The Soviet Union threatened to take sides with Egypt. The United States, fearing the spread of Soviet power in the region, pressured Britain, France and Israel into agreeing to a cease-fire. By Christmas 1956 the Brits had been withdrawn. The great Anglo-French imperial adventure ended in national humiliation, which bitterly divided this nation. The British prime minister, Anthony Eden, was shattered by the Suez experience and resigned a few weeks later.For the Allies the casualties were light. Britain suffered 16 killed, France 10 and Israel 189. But more than 2,600 Egyptian soldiers and civilians lost their lives in the Suez operation, and thousands more lost their homes and suffered near-starvation.

Etched forever in the memory of Ken Chambers is 23 August 1956. 'I was twenty-two and I'd been out of the army for two years,' he recalls at his home in West Bromwich. 'Suddenly I got this telegram. I thought it was a practical joke at first but with a War Office stamp and my army details on it. It read, "Please report within 48 hours to Coopers Lane Camp, CAD Bramley, Hampshire. Railway warrant attached." We sailed out of Famagusta docks on a converted merchant ship. As we sailed into Port Said we could see smoke billowing from the town. We landed near to the docks to the sound of small-arms fire coming from the forward units clearing remnants of the Egyptian forces from around the town. I can recall seeing the sunken ships Nasser had instructed to be sunk to block the entrance of the Canal. Our task was to offload ammunition and create a supply depot, which we achieved about 3 miles outside the port. We commandeered an old market-place that was a good defensive site for our operating headquarters. We were hungry most of the time, and tinned sausages and bacon never tasted so good. The forty-eight-hour packs we were issued with were our lifeline. We made the best of old fruit baskets and mosquito nets to get some kip. Then came the withdrawal. We coped with that OK, loading ammunition onto trucks and convoying it to waiting ships at Port Said, and we moved 400 tons without incident. At the same time we noticed UN troops were more active. One morning on parade we were given the good news that we would be home for Christmas.'

As the invasion gathered pace Syd Wheat, a twenty-one-year-old leading mechanical engineer in the Royal Navy, watched as his ship, the aircraft carrier HMS *Bulwark*, sent Sea Hawk jets into the attack. 'It was a very busy forty-eight hours. But we didn't lose a single aircraft.'

Flying jets from aircraft carriers was in its infancy. At his home in Lichfield Syd recalls the build-up to the operation, with *Bulwark* calling at dry dock in Gibraltar to have her bottom scraped of barnacles and repainted. 'She needed all the speed she could get for the jets to take-off. They wanted to get her up to about 28 knots. We had an inkling something was going on because of what we saw in the papers. There were French ships with us and the American fleet shadowing us just over the horizon.'

Did he and his shipmates have any reservations about the operation? 'No. I served for twelve years and in those days what the government said we had to obey. It wasn't like nowadays with everyone running around like headless chickens. We just got on with the job. We didn't give much thought to the rights and wrongs. If it was in the interests of Great Britain then it was a case of let's do it. When you're twenty-one you don't really think of things like that. Looking back, I am proud to have taken part and to have done my bit for Queen and Country – although I do think we were a bit heavy-handed.'

Mick Schofield of Coseley was a nineteen-year-old army medic with a grandstand view of the Suez invasion. 'On the night of 5 November I was standing on the front rail of HMS *Theseus* watching the strike aircraft from HMS *Eagle* attacking the installations on shore with rockets and guns. It didn't seem real. It was like watching a Hollywood war film. I don't think I slept that night, I was too absorbed. The next morning at daybreak the helicopters moved the commandos to the shore. There was no let-up in the attack all during the night, and the next day with explosives, gunfire and shellfire. The helicopters were going back and forth with their loads of commandos; one of them on the return flight crashed into the drink. Two teams of about six medics were detailed to collect the dead bodies along our sector. This they did using, as I recollect, a school bus and a Pepsi Cola lorry. Myself and around another eight medics were ordered to set up a burial party. When the dead arrived we were told to dig mass graves as there were about eighty to a hundred bodies of the enemy to bury. We buried, with due respect, the bodies in these two graves. These soldiers seemed to be dressed in the same kind of battledress as our own, and I could not help thinking that their army had made use of stores that we had perhaps left behind after the end of the Second World War.'John Owen of Bentley, Walsall, was a teenage sailor on HMS *Alamein*, in the thick of the fighting from the first day of the Suez attack. 'The place was absolutely full of bullet holes. There had been a real battle.' While ashore he took a photograph of the statue of Ferdinand de Lesseps, the engineer who built the Suez Canal. It turned out to be one of the last snaps of a hated symbol of foreign domination, which had stood for fifty -seven years. A few days later, on Christmas Eve 1956, a crowd of Egyptians surrounded the 40-foot statue, placed explosives between the stone pedestal and the bronze figure of the canal builder and, to wild cheering, blew it up. On the next day, Christmas Day, HMS *Alamein* steamed proudly into Malta. 'I am glad to have been part of it. We were asked to do our duty and we did everything that was required of us.'Mick Drury of Hednesford was a twenty-year-old fitter with the Royal Engineers and arrived in the wake of a bloody assault by the Parachute Regiment. 'We sighted Egypt the following afternoon. There seemed to be lots of burning buildings in the port area and some rifle fire and small explosions, but nothing to worry us. The airborne troops had landed earlier. There were other military vessels and a troop ship in the docks. Our job was to clear any damaged vehicles from the road system and, using tank ships, pull down heavily damaged buildings. On the first day's work in the dock we were told to push several badly damaged lorries into the water at the entrance to the canal. Then a lieutenant-colonel went mad at us, saying we were blocking water they would need to land other vessels.'

John Bentley was a nineteen-year-old National Serviceman from Bloxwich who went ashore at Port Said in a tank landing craft. He saw the bodies of Egyptian soldiers slumped over their guns where they had died in the initial attack by paratroops. 'I had never seen dead bodies before. Me and a pal sat beside the canal for our lunch when this body came drifting past with one leg missing. It was a dead Egyptian. A few minutes later his leg came floating past. Suddenly we didn't feel like eating. I had nightmares for a long time afterwards.'

As the Suez Crisis deepened in the summer of 1956 Private 23173937 Bentley of the North Staffordshire Regiment had been one of thousands of young British soldiers massing in camps for the invasion. 'We were at Aldershot and no-one told us where we were going. But when we saw the tanks being repainted the colour of the desert sand we knew where it was. I didn't really understand what it was about. People were talking about Britain keeping the canal.'

As a 'general dogsbody' attached to a corps headquarters, he recalls marching through Port Said with a loaded rifle and fixed bayonets as sniper fire crackled around. 'You can imagine how we felt. We were told to spend the night wherever we could. The first night was in a garage, the second in a hotel cellar full of rats. But after that time became meaningless.' He was in Egypt for several weeks, eventually arriving home in Bloxwich in time for Christmas. 'I had my rifle and my pack and I was absolutely shattered,' says John. 'Wolves were playing and there was a huge queue for the Bloxwich bus but everyone let me go to the front. It was like a hero's return.' *November 2006*

Testing the nuclear deterrent

'We faced away from the explosion. We wore sunglasses and we covered our eyes with our hands. When it went off, we could see our finger bones,' says Roger Carter. 'There was a lorry nearby and we thought we'd get on it for a better view. Then we saw the blast knocking over the palm trees in front of us. Then it knocked us flat, too. There was this wave of heat and this enormous turmoil of red, black and gold burning in the sky. Some people say it was beautiful. It was certainly awe-inspiring.' Roger Carter, a twenty-two-year-old NCO in 49 Squadron, was witnessing hell on earth. Thousands of British servicemen saw one or two nuclear explosions as observers (some say guinea pigs) at the UK tests in the Pacific and the Australian Outback. But Roger, who led the team responsible for loading and handling these fearsome devices, saw six tests – three atom bombs and three hydrogen bombs. The one that knocked him off his feet on Christmas Island sticks in his mind. So does the infernal aftermath of an A-bomb in Australia. 'I have gazed into the hole made by an atom bomb, which, in retrospect, was perhaps a stupid thing to do. There were old aircraft around and lots of black glass caused by the sand melting. It was a pretty horrific sight.'

But the emotion that comes echoing down the decades is neither awe nor horror but pride. The RAF's 49 Squadron, created specifically to drop the first atom and hydrogen bombs, was an exclusive little club. 'We had tremendous pride in the squadron. There was wonderful camaraderie and it was a very democratic unit.'Thirty members of the squadron held their last Megaton Club reunion at Cosford RAF Museum in 2007. 'We decided to make it the last because we didn't want to go on until there were only two of us left.'

The paranoia and secrecy of the Cold War is easily forgotten. Roger Carter recalls how the devices, powerful enough to destroy a city, were kept under green tarpaulins, away from prying eyes. Under the wraps, he found himself face to face with the hardware of Armageddon. 'It was a big bugger. It was fairly streamlined and painted dark green. I think we were more scared of the Americans than the Russians. If anyone had managed to get a picture of the device the Americans could say we were a security risk.'For Squadron Leader Arthur Steele, commander of the Valiant which dropped the third hydrogen bomb, the experience was deeply sobering. 'When you have released, the number-one requirement is to get the hell out of there. We turned our tail to the detonation and there were steel shutters over all the windows. We didn't see the flash but there were two positive thumps as the shockwaves hit us, one from the detonation, the other reflected from the sea.'Mr Steele, who flew Mosquito bombers in the Second World War, is immensely proud to have taken part in the nuclear tests, the biggest combined-services operation since the war. He witnessed several of the test explosions. 'They were incredibly impressive, not in a "Wow, that's great!" sort of way but in the sense that these are dreadful weapons and for God's sake let's be bright enough never to have to use them. People who were involved in the V-bombers were not gung-ho about clobbering anyone. We just prayed that we could keep the Cold War from going hot until the Soviet Union broke down from within, which is what happened. We tried to convince the Soviets that they should not do anything stupid – and it worked.'

The ultimate question is plain. If the order had come, would the young professional RAF crews have dropped these infernal weapons? 'It's a difficult thing to contemplate. But if it had got to that stage the crews were trained, they had a job to do, and they would have done the best they could.'It is a bleak moment. Roger Carter lightens the mood. He laughs as he recalls the member of 49 Squadron with a forlorn-hope sort of job as the Valiants hurtled off to deliver their terrible cargoes. 'He was called Bill, and he was poised at the far end of the runway with a petrol-driven cutting machine. If the plane crashed his job was to cut a hole in it so the security officer could get in and disarm the bomb. Assuming he could get his machine started.' *June 2007*

Vietnam
In Cambodia the smell told him when to start filming. It was the stench of the Killing Fields. In the Gulf War he limited himself to filming

twenty or fifty bodies at a time. He could have filmed thousands in one batch, piled 10 feet high. Yet in nearly four decades of filming the vilest scenes of man's inhumanity, only two wars deeply affected Erik Durschmied. The first was the Second World War, when he was fourteen and Allied bombs rained down on his native Vienna. 'Your own war is always different. If bombs fall on your house or someone puts a bomb in a pub in Birmingham, of course it concerns you in a very special way.' The second was Vietnam. 'It affected me because I spoke the same language as the soldiers. You would be maybe talking to a helicopter pilot before a flight, sharing a beer and then, all of a sudden, bang, he's dead. I saw more bodies in Iran and Iraq. They were everywhere. It was unimaginable. We simply couldn't show the real horror of it.' Yet it is Vietnam that has marked his soul. From 1960 to 1972 he was Panorama's top cameraman, dutifully reporting a war that began with the best of intentions and degenerated into an aimless, brutal, national disgrace that tore America apart. Even today the United States can barely face what happened in Vietnam. Durschmied traces the trauma to January 1968 when the Viet Cong launched its Tet offensive. Thanks to news cameramen like him, American viewers witnessed their young soldiers dying in action and saw enemy guerillas inside the US embassy in Saigon. It was a shattering blow to morale. Today the pundits claim that Tet marked the last desperate fling of the Viet Cong and was an American military victory. 'We have a word for that – balls. It may have been a military victory but it was a total political defeat.'

Even today veterans are shunned. For every limbless ex-GI there are a dozen with nightmares and mental problems from the most harrowing of wars. 'At least in the Second World War you knew when you reached the Reichstag it was over. All the enmity could be directed against the enemy. But in Vietnam, from '68 onwards, all the enmity was turned inwards on the States with the riots, the Black Panthers and everything. The Americans are good soldiers, they think for themselves. But after '68 they didn't believe in what they were fighting for.' From Vietnam Erik moved on to Aden, Rhodesia, the Middle East, Afghanistan and Cambodia, making a good living from the very worst of human behaviour. Combat has left him with no nightmares, he insists, and no illusions about luck. 'Luck is a thick brick wall. There's nothing else. Whether you live or die depends on which side of the wall you are.' *April 1990*

In the tunnels of Cu Chi

The tunnels of Cu Chi extend for about 200 miles. After 10 yards I'd had enough: 10 feet underground the tunnel is so narrow it brushes your sides, so low you are bent double. The way both forward and back is blocked by other people. The tunnel widens into an old Vietcong conference room. It steadily fills with trippers until we are standing, sweating, shoulder to shoulder. The only way out is another panicky, heart-thumping crawl into the rat-run of tunnels. A bat suddenly flickers through the gloom. You duck. A woman gasps in alarm. Your chest tightens from belly to throat. Know the enemy. And if your darkest enemy is claustrophobia, then give the tunnels of Cu Chi a miss. Yet even in the narrowest, lowest part of this section, you are not experiencing a fraction of the horrors of this place. Throw in the type of warfare that went on down here, the shooting, spearing, knife-fighting and booby traps, all in the pitch black, and you are into the stuff of nightmares. The tunnels on show today have been specially enlarged for the tourists. Originally they were scooped out, with trowel and wicker basket, no more than a couple of feet high. The slender jungle fighters of the Vietcong (VC) could slip through with ease; the big-boned Yanks stuck fast. At least that was the theory as the VC dug ever deeper and further. Eventually the tunnels extended from the Cu Chi district, 30 miles north of Saigon, to the very gates of the city. They are on three levels, the deepest more than 30 feet below ground. Armouries and operating theatres were constructed. Kitchens worked around the clock, the tell-tale smoke dispersed through a cunning colander of vents. 'See it here? Look again,' smiles our Vietnam Army guide. Beneath a pile of leaves in the dappled jungle a chimney barely as wide as a finger produces a thin trail of acrid blue smoke from the charcoal cooker below. Entrances were hidden beneath camouflaged steel trap doors or dug into river banks below river level. By day the Vietcong rested or sneaked out to work their paddy fields. By night they emerged from their secret tunnels and gave the Yankees hell.

From the mid-1960s the US Army knew there were tunnels, but even the most intensive searches failed to find more than a few trapdoors, baited with landmines to kill the intruder. When the Yanks sent down sniffer dogs the VC began using stolen US soap and combat jackets to hide their alien scent. The unfortunate US 25th Division unwittingly built its headquarters on top of the tunnels and suffered dreadful losses as the Vietcong emerged, machine-gunned the Americans' tents and blew up their helicopters. The Communists foraged for US weapons. After every air strike or artillery bombardment they would seek out unexploded shells and bombs, sawing them open, often with fatal consequences, to use the precious explosives in home-made grenades and rockets. They even perfected a mine, triggered by the swaying palm branches, to destroy helicopter gunships. So secure felt the VC that ceremonies were held underground to present medals to those who killed Americans and destroyed tanks. There were cultural events with dancers and singers smuggled down from North Vietnam to entertain the troops.

The US response was to form the Tunnel Rats, a volunteer unit of small, dedicated soldiers who braved the furthest recesses of this awful place to play 'Charlie' at his own game. 'See here,' says the guide. In the corner of the underground command cell is a 10-foot pit, razor-sharp bamboo stakes in the bottom. 'When the American found a room he always went into the corner: it was the best place to fight from. So we dug these,' the soldier smiles. The Americans always tried to recover their dead or wounded Tunnel Rats, tugging them out with a rope around the feet. The Vietcong responded by lying in wait where the tunnels widened into rooms. As the Tunnel Rat stuck his head in the waiting VC would skewer him through the neck with a bamboo spear, trapping the body forever. Other traps included grenades on trip wires and hollow tubes containing spiders, scorpions, poisonous snakes – and worse. There were many awful ways to die in 'Nam but could anything rival the agony and wretchedness of one Tunnel Rat, choked to death by a boa constrictor in a VC trap?

From the tunnels of Cu Chi the Vietcong planned, equipped and launched their 1968 Tet offensive on Saigon and other major cities. Suddenly the black-pyjama guerillas were everywhere. At this stage fiction takes over from fact in the all-pervading propaganda dished out to today's thin but growing trickle of tourists. If you believe everything they tell you at Cu Chi, the Americans were defeated by a popular uprising among the people. It wasn't quite like that. The VC guerillas who streamed out of Cu Chi expected the city-folk of Saigon to rally to their support. It didn't happen. Tet was a military disaster for the Communists. The US Embassy takeover, described by one American officer as 'a piddling platoon action', was repulsed in a matter of hours. The Viet Cong lost forty thousand in Tet and was so badly mauled that it never again fought a pitched battle.

Worse was to follow. Cu Chi was razed by huge US bulldozers, its trees stripped bare with defoliant chemicals. The US dropped tons of 'American grass' seed, producing a tinder-dry crop which was then ignited from the air. Cu Chi was declared a free-fire zone. Anything that moved was attacked. Warplanes returning with unused bombs were told to drop them on Cu Chi. Finally, when the mighty B-52 bombers were no longer being used against the North, they set about carpet-bombing Cu Chi. Where the Tunnel Rats had failed, 1,000-pound, delayed-action bombs succeeded. Vast sections of the maze were destroyed.

Of the sixteen thousand guerillas who fought from Cu Chi, ten thousand were killed. But that was not the point. The men and women who lived and died in these tunnels may have been beaten in military terms but they won an overwhelming victory for hearts and minds. For after Tet the American public gave up all hope of winning the war. In the very week of the offensive the tally of American dead in Vietnam passed that of the Korean War, traumatising the nation. In all, fifty thousand Americans were to die here. The anti-war movement grew. Richard Nixon was elected on the pledge of bringing the boys home. Later the North Vietnamese Army, assisted by the remnants of the Vietcong, invaded the South and took over.

Today the tunnels of Cu Chi are tranquil, surrounded by an eerie forest of saplings and American grass. The enemy's old bombs and shells are museum pieces. Bomb-craters are signposted and displayed with pride, like war wounds. And here and there, from vents deep-hidden in the leaf mould, come the gasps of tourists deep below. Amazement, admiration, panic. *November 1993*

A Porton Down guinea pig

It was the chauffeur-driven car that really shook him. Aged twenty-four, Tony Levy was just another bored young squaddie looking for a change of scenery and some extra money. The offer on the notice board at 10 Signal Regiment in London looked too good to miss. The Ministry of Defence wanted volunteers for the world-famous chemical warfare establishment at Porton Down in Wiltshire. The lure was an extra week's pay. Signalman Levy signed up. When he stepped out of the station at Salisbury, he got a VIP reception. 'There was this black staff car and a chauffeur waiting for me,' he recalls. 'That threw me a bit.' Behind the barbed wire at Porton Down he was one of hundreds of young servicemen who were used as guinea pigs in Britain's chemical and germ -warfare research. He says he is still suffering the side-effects. Now a civilian and married with six children, he says, 'I have a general distrust of the medical profession. Anyway, I'm hale and hearty and I have achieved my aims.'

But he is not the man he was. A change came over him within days of leaving Porton Down and returning to his barracks. 'It looked like a collection of old Nissen huts, with side wards. I was taken to an individual bed space and ten minutes later I was surrounded by white coats, measured and had blood and urine samples taken. They shaved my head and fixed electrodes leading to a socket which hung behind me like a pony tail.' He was given tablets every six hours. Every four hours a blood sample was taken. Tony Levy says he was told the tablets were atropine, a substance derived from deadly nightshade which is used to fight the effects of nerve gas. In fact, the file at Porton Down reveals he was actually dosed with P2S, pralidoxime mesylate. This is a chemical now used, in conjunction with atropine, in the automatic syringe issued in every British soldier's chemical warfare kit. He says the effects on him have been startling and permanent. 'At first I didn't realise what was happening. Army life is full of periods of excitement followed by boredom. Then I realised I was becoming hyperactive. Before Porton Down I was just the average skiving squaddie. Afterwards I began rushing around. I got a reputation for being fast and efficient. The downside is that I can't sit still for more than ten minutes. Over Christmas I couldn't relax to watch a single film. It's crazy. At this time of life most of my contemporaries are laid-back but I'm not. I can't cool down or chill out.'For fifty years, from 1940 to 1990, volunteers took part in NBC (nuclear, biological and chemical) warfare tests at Porton Down. During the Cold War few questioned the need for such research. The former Soviet Union was armed to the teeth with nerve gas, blister-causing chemicals and a host of other battlefield poisons. At home in Wednesfield, Tony Levy reflects with his usual breathless urgency on his time at Porton Down. 'At the time I was on £25 a week. I wanted some more money. I did my bit for Queen and country, but now I wish I had never gone near the place.' *January 2003*

Cold War warriors
No uniforms. No use of rank. No military vehicles. They were curious orders for an army exercise. The civilian minibus driver must have wondered what was going on when he dropped a dozen of us off in the middle of nowhere, next to what looked like a deserted factory depot. It was the summer of 1980. I was a Territorial Army officer commanding a Royal Signals troop whose war-role was to survive the nuclear attack, restore communications and 'assist the civil authorities in the recovery period'. At that time the Cold War was more bitter than ever. Whitehall was about to re-publish *Protect and Survive*, a leaflet explaining how Joe Public could live through nuclear war by putting kitchen foil over the windows and hiding under the stairs. Our hiding place was rather more substantial. When the minibus had left we made our way inside the Regional Seat of Government bunker at Wolverley, near Kidderminster, known to us simply as 'The Hole'. It was breathtaking. From vast central corridors hewn out of the rock, side galleries ran endlessly into the darkness. A quarter of a million square feet, hidden 200 feet beneath Kinver Edge. There was a huge, clattering kitchen area, sleeping accommodation, a mass dormitory, officials' quarters, rest-rooms, showers, lavatories and radiation decontamination rooms. 'The Hole' was constructed during the Second World War as a shadow factory where aero engines were produced, safe from Nazi bombing. Mothballed at the end of the war, it found a new role during the Cold War.

Our week-long exercise brought together government scientists, police, fire and ambulance chiefs and local council officials (who rather spoiled things by going home at 5pm sharp every evening). My troop provided the communications, manning a bank of dusty, ancient Creed teleprinters and an equally venerable Marconi radio. The regional controller, who would have had wartime powers of life and death over every citizen in Nine Region (West Midlands, Warwickshire, Shropshire, Staffordshire and Hereford and Worcester) was played by a senior civil servant from Whitehall called Raymond. Raymond was a hoot. A product of public school and Oxbridge, he threw himself into the drama like a cross between Winston Churchill and Abraham Lincoln. When he heard he had his very own radio troop, he retired to his office and drafted a public broadcast to the fireballed, irradiated and possibly lawless citizenry of Nine Region. It ran to about eight pages and was pitched somewhere between the Gettysburg Address and Blue Birds Over the White Cliffs of Dover. It was a stirring call to stand firm, think of England, keep your pecker up and listen out for further instructions, coupled with the hint that any mutiny would be dealt with pretty damn quick. 'Will you tell him, or shall I?' asked my troop sergeant, brandishing the missive. I did it, breaking the news to the regional controller that, actually, it wasn't that sort of wireless. People couldn't tune in to Hole Radio. It was a teleprinter link, and anyway we couldn't send real names and locations.'So what can you send?' Raymond asked earnestly. 'Well, usually we send radio checks and signal strengths. Although, to be honest, the set doesn't often work.' Unable to address his public, Raymond returned to making decisions about whether to use firing squads on them. He never slept. Day or night, Raymond stayed alert and constantly busy. Two hundred feet underground you tend to get day and night confused, so we came to rely on Raymond: if he had his slippers on it was night. By the end of the exercise I had developed a profound respect for senior civil servants and a deep depression about the prospect of nuclear war. In the fluorescent-lit bunker, breathing purified air and drinking recycled water, the gap between exercise and reality narrowed. When a request for 20,000 cardboard coffins for Stourbridge came through, the TA soldier next to me who was from Stourbridge got up and walked away, red-faced, blinking hard. It was, in technical terms, a 'good' exercise. The radio worked well and hundreds of messages were passed. And yet when the final 'ENDEX' clattered over the teleprinter, the relief was awesome. We switched off, tidied up and went out through the huge steel door, drawing in great, grateful lungfuls of fresh air. We were told the location was top secret. But was it? Before the exercise one of our TA sergeants drove to Wolverley to make quite sure we found 'The Hole' on the day. He got lost and stopped a passer-by to ask directions to Wolverley. 'You looking for the secret place?' inquired the local. That's how secret

Number Nine Regional Seat of Government really was. And those of us who worked there strongly suspected that, if the warheads had started flying, one of the first would have had Wolverley written all over it. *August 1993*

'The Hole' revisited

It is like the opening scene of *Titanic*. A single beam of light penetrates the blackness, like the robot camera 6 miles deep probing the stricken liner's cabins. A collapsed pile of timber comes into view, festooned with dry rot as thick as a snowdrift. All is decay, darkness and silence. At this point in the movie the rusting sunken hulk of *Titanic* suddenly comes to life. At this point in my trip I recall the summer of 1980 when this dying, echoing place was full of life, noise and purpose. It seems like yesterday. From the canteen came the cheerful smell of bacon as dozens of pairs of cutlery clattered. The corridors were thronged with soldiers, scientists and civilians moving back and forth as we rehearsed for Armageddon. For this is 'The Hole', the nuclear bunker deep beneath Kinver Edge at Wolverley where, if the worst happened, a small group of experts would manage the survival and recovery of what would be known as Nine Region.

As a lad growing up in Kinver, Paul Stokes knew there was something secret under the Edge. But locals kept tight-lipped. According to whispered folklore there was a massive bunker on several levels, like something out of a James Bond film. 'A lot of people knew the secrets of this place and kept quiet,' he says as he unlocks a solid steel door and enters the bunker. 'Even today we find that people who worked here are reluctant to talk about it. They just feel they shouldn't.'

It's hardly surprising. Drakelow, as the complex is generally known, was built in extreme secrecy early in the Second World War. Five vast tunnels were blasted deep into the sandstone cliff. More than 6 million cubic feet of stone was scooped out. By 1942 the underground complex was a 'shadow' Rover factory, turning out the equivalent of fifteen thousand aero engines for the war against Germany.

Paul switches on the diesel generator. Light floods the tunnels. Wartime notices and 1940s clocks and Tannoy speakers still hang from the whitewashed walls and ceilings. You can almost hear the distant strains of Workers' Playtime.

After the war Drakelow became an even bigger secret. As the Cold War between Russia and the West simmered, Regional Seats of Government were created all over Britain. By 1990 the Cold War was over and the regional bunkers were sold off by the Home Office. In 1993 Paul Stokes and a friend cheekily posed as potential buyers and were allowed in to inspect the place. The big secret of his childhood was laid bare. Not some James Bond super-bunker, but the crudely blasted tunnels of total warfare. Soon afterwards Drakelow passed into the hands of a private company. Paul Stokes and a few pals formed The Friends of Drakelow Tunnels and now spend their spare time running guided tours, keeping an eye on the place and doing maintenance. It is an uphill struggle against nature. Some other nuclear bunkers have been preserved as museums; the wartime tunnels beneath Dover Castle are rightly regarded as a national treasure; Churchill's war rooms deep beneath Whitehall have just been refurbished; and yet Drakelow crumbles.

'It's not right,' says Paul. 'This place is unique. None of the other bunkers have the history, going right back to the last war.' As he raises funds and tries to stimulate interest in this national treasure, he smiles at how old legends never die. To this day you still find people who are convinced there's a lot more here than you can see. They still think it has five levels with secret lifts. There's a persistent rumour that thousands of cardboard coffins are stored here. Well, I've been all over the place and I've never seen them yet.' *February 2005*

CHAPTER FIVE
THE FALKLANDS

Into battle

War? It was every cliché you can think of, says Roger Goodwin. 'There was no warning. I just heard something going dacka-dacka-dacka. There was this frozen moment. We just looked at each other. I suddenly realised it was a machine-gun going off. So I shouted "hit the deck!" Just like something out of a John Wayne movie. Can you believe it? Hit the deck?'

Over a steak sandwich in a Wolverhampton wine bar, Goodwin roars with laughter at the madness of Bomb Alley. He was an Ministry of Defence press 'minder' in the Falklands War. Under fire for the first time, he hit the deck in the bowels of an ammunition ship in San Carlos Water. For twenty minutes as Argentinian warplanes strafed and bombed, he examined the carpet and analysed his feelings. 'I remember quite coldly thinking "how do I feel?" I wasn't scared. I was elated, excited and fatalistic. There was a heightening of all your sensations, an alertness, an astuteness. The sky was bluer, the colours sharper. There were a load of schoolboy emotions. I remember it going through my head like a piece of ticker-tape, they don't pay civil servants to do this.'

At thirty-nine, Roger Goodwin was the Navy's duty public-relations man in Whitehall on the 'fairly quiet night' of 1–2 April 1982. Suddenly 'all hell broke loose' as news came in of the Argentinian invasion. Goodwin was sent south on HMS *Invincible* as minder to five Fleet Street reporters. He frankly admits there were two wars, one against the Argentinians, the other against journalists who brought peacetime practices to the business of war reporting. Sharing an 18,000-ton warship with five news-hungry hacks and Prince Andrew was not an enviable experience. There were lighter moments, as when the Prince spoofed the *Sun* with a yarn about how he relaxed in force nine gales by playing pool on a gyro-stabilised table. No stranger to Fleet Street, Goodwin was shocked at the behaviour, and the naïvety, of some of his charges, especially their belief that it would not come to a shooting war. 'I'm no great political analyst but why couldn't they see that here were two right-wing politicians who had painted themselves into a corner, and if either side blinked their government would fall?'

A total of 252 British servicemen died in the Falklands War and 777 were wounded. Argentina lost 635 dead and more than 1,000 were wounded. The heaviest losses on both sides happened at sea: there were 197 British deaths at sea or on ships bombed in Falkland harbours; Argentine naval losses were 356, including 323 on the *General Belgrano*.After the surrender on 14 June 1982 British forces took 12,978 Argentinians as prisoners of war. All were repatriated between 18 June and 14 July. Three days after the surrender the Argentinian leader General Leopoldo Galtieri resigned. The military junta collapsed in 1983.

When victory came Goodwin sent a telegram not to his wife, Wendy, but to his parents, 'because mothers worry. It was just a string of words, a jumble of emotions. Happy, elated, proud.' *April 1992*

The sinking of the *Belgrano*

They had trained, trained and trained again. In May 1982 the crew of Her Majesty's Submarine *Conqueror* were part of a silent, elite force. They were deep in the South Atlantic, tracking a warship whose name was soon to pass into history. 'None of us had been to war before,' says Steve McIntosh from Bilston. 'It was just like another exercise when we went to action stations.'The submarine had been tracking the Argentinian cruiser *General Belgrano* for days. On board *Conqueror*, Steve was a seventeen-year-old contact evaluation plotter in the control room. 'All the information was getting relayed back to the government in London. We did ask permission to engage her and we were knocked back several times.'

Finally Whitehall authorised *Belgrano*'s destruction. 'We were carrying wire-guided torpedoes but we decided to use Mk 8s, the Second World War torpedo, fired in salvoes of three. We could hear everything. We could feel the submarine shake slightly as they were fired. We could hear them running for a while and then everything went silent. Then we heard two impacts. It was like a thud and a hollow clap, and a weird tinkling. That was the metal of the ship breaking up. There was also the smell of cordite coming back up the torpedo tubes. At first the mood was fantastic. But when it sank in we thought what have we done? Although we were at war it wasn't as though we thought about the enemy as people. The *Belgrano* was a big and very, very dangerous ship. We knew we had to disarm it, to make sure there was no confrontation with the Task Force. 'It became the most controversial event in the Falklands War. The *Belgrano* went down with the loss of 323 lives, the single biggest death toll of the campaign. A ferocious debate began and has never ended. Some claim the warship was heading away from the combat area and was no threat. Others argue that the *Belgrano* was the southern part of a pincer movement by the Argentinian navy, which could have decimated the British fleet. One thing is certain. Once she was sunk the Argentinian navy fled the seas for the rest of the war. For Steve McIntosh, the operation secured him a place in history. He has the distinction of being the first black sailor ever to have served on a Royal Navy submarine when it sank another vessel in war. He was following a family tradition. Born to Jamaican parents in Sedgley, he grew up in Bilston and was educated at Moseley Park School. His older brother David and twin brother Clive both served in submarines but Steve was the only one to see action. Steve says HMS *Conqueror* earlier had the Argentinian flagship, the aircraft carrier *Veinticinco de Mayo*, in her sights. Sinking the carrier might have shortened the war and been an even bigger bloodbath than the *Belgrano* attack. He says the British government refused permission to engage.

After the 2 May attack on the *Belgrano* the British submarine went 'fast and deep' to avoid the cruiser's smaller escort ships. 'Later on there was a service on board. We prayed for those who had been left behind by their escorts.' Does he have any regrets about sinking the *Belgrano*? 'I was very young and I didn't push the button. We were all part of a team. We trained all the time. On the sub it was very clear. I thought it was a shame that people lost their lives but I still think it was either them or us. I felt sorry for their sailors because they were conscripts. No way were they as good as we were.'

Two days after the sinking of the *Belgrano* the destroyer HMS *Sheffield* was destroyed by an Argentinian missile. *Sheffield* was the first Royal Navy ship to be sunk in action since the Second World War. Blood had been spilled on both sides. Hope of a peaceful solution in the Falklands was fading fast. *May 2007*

HMS *Glasgow*

Martin White of Wednesbury was a twenty-year-old radar operator on *Sheffield*'s sister ship, HMS *Glasgow* and saw *Sheffield*'s destruction. 'We had seen videos of Exocets in training so we knew what to expect,' he recalls. 'Seeing *Sheffield* on fire was terrible.' Eight days later *Glasgow* was in the thick of it. Martin was on duty in the ship's war room as Argentinian warplanes attacked. 'You could hear bombs going off and guns firing, and missiles misfiring. We had just come from missile training without any problems. But when you really needed them the missiles failed. It was scary, very scary. And suddenly there was this thump.'Hours later the ship's company were told that the thump was an enemy bomb which had struck *Glasgow* but passed straight through the ship without exploding or causing any injuries. By the time the war was over the damaged ship was heading home to a heroes' reception. Cheering crowds lined the docks at Portsmouth. 'I don't think there was a single member of the crew not on deck. It was a nice reaction, the thanks of the people of the UK. Looking back, I am glad to have done it, and very, very proud of taking part.'

Back on dry land, Martin White raced north to make his younger brother's wedding in Yorkshire. He turned up unexpectedly in his best uniform 'and everyone was in tears'. As the reception ended he went to pick up his navy hat. He found it resting on a bottle of champagne.
March 2007

Blinded on HMS *Antrim*

The last thing Terry Bullingham ever saw was two Argentinian Mirage jets, head-on.

'It was like an air show,' he recalls at his Smethwick home. 'They were so low and going too fast to register properly. Then there was a sound like calico ripping, only many times louder.' It was the roar of the warplanes opening fire with their cannon. Shells exploded around the flight deck of the Royal Navy destroyer HMS *Antrim*.Chief Petty Officer Bullingham felt 'a sickening blow' and, at the age of thirty-seven, his world went black. It was 21 May 1982. HMS *Antrim*, providing air defence for the troopship *Canberra*, had been struck by two Argentinian bombs which failed to explode. Next came a strafing attack, which left a cluster of crew injured and CPO Bullingham blinded. 'We heard this huge metallic ring as the bomb struck. We didn't know whether it had gone off or not. We were busy cooling the decks with water. Then we saw the Mirages. I was hit in the arms and leg. I remember going into the foetal position. Someone said, "You've got a couple of black eyes," and I thought, he's lying.'Terry Bullingham is relentlessly upbeat. If you have to be blinded, he says, it's far better to lose it instantly. 'It just went black. No shades of grey. No flashes of light. No anxiety. Nothing to distract your brain. Just total blackness and two plastic eyes. Now you see it, now you don't.'He works for St Dunstan's, the charity caring for those in the armed forces and emergency services who are blinded in the service of their country. Driven by his wife, Maria, he travels the Midlands speaking to community groups about the work of St Dunstan's and 'breaking down barriers' between the sighted and non-sighted. He jokes a lot. He says he has never felt despair. He stayed in the Navy for two years after the Falklands War, working as a guide at a navy museum.

'I could have stayed on. But that would have been the comfortable thing. I didn't want to end up as the old fart at the end of the mess bar. I've never had any problems with the politics of it. Think what would have happened if we'd just left it and done nothing. I'm glad I took part because the people in the Navy who didn't take part still feel guilty. But I don't think people realise how lucky we were. The Argentinians had four submarines and we had no idea where they were. Supposing they had sunk three of our ships. The whole thing was luck.' *March 2002*

Waiting for an Exocet to strike

It's the word any sailor in the 1982 Falklands War came to dread. 'Handbrake!' was the operations-room warning of an Exocet missile attack. On board HMS *Exeter* on 25 May Steve Stonard and his comrades froze for a split-second as the electronic-warfare operator shouted the word. 'It meant that the Exocet's signal had locked on to us,' recalls the former sailor. Someone blew a whistle and we threw ourselves to the deck.'

No-one on HMS *Exeter* had any illusions. An identical Type 42 destroyer, HMS *Sheffield*, had already been destroyed by an Exocet. 'We were very busy all the time. I remember long periods when nothing seemed to happen. But you could almost set your watch by the air raids.'

The job of the Type 42s was to defend the aircraft carriers at the heart of the British fleet. If that meant taking hits, so be it. For a desperate few seconds as the Exocet approached, Leading Seaman Stonard, a twenty-six-year-old sonar operator, and his shipmates waited for the impact. And waited. It never came. The destroyer's defence system had fired a cloud of metallic strips known as 'chaff', deflecting the missile.

Nearby, the huge cargo vessel *Atlantic Conveyor* was not so lucky. Two Exocets struck her, wrecking the ship, writing off vast quantities of equipment and claiming twenty lives, including that of Wolverhampton sailor Adrian Anslow. HMS *Exeter* survived the South Atlantic conflict unscathed and a quarter-century later was the only Falklands ship still serving with the Royal Navy. 'Which is remarkable when you think how small the Navy is today,' smiles the ex-sailor, living in Bartley Green, Birmingham.

The war ended suddenly when Argentine forces surrendered to the British in Port Stanley. By then another Type 42 destroyer, HMS *Coventry*, had been destroyed by bombs. Britain lost twenty-one ships sunk or damaged. If all the Argentinian unexploded bombs had detonated correctly the fleet would have been decimated.

'The surrender was a bit surreal. The captain announced over the ship's Tannoy that it had taken place. People were very relieved to hear it. We were pleased but, of course, for those of us in the Navy there was also a great sense of loss.'

Steve Stonard joined the Royal Navy aged sixteen in 1973. He served until 1984, followed by seventeen years in the Royal Naval Reserve. While some 1980s servicemen never expected to go to war, he was a veteran of the 1975 Cod War with Iceland, which saw some deliberate rammings in a dispute over fisheries. When the Falklands conflict erupted in the spring of 1982 HMS *Exeter* was based in the West Indies and looking forward to a peaceful cruise home to Britain. Then came the summons south. When it was over the destroyer was one of the first into Port Stanley. 'It was a mess. There was ammunition and missiles scattered all over the place.' *June 2007*

The furious Colonel H. Jones
In the half-light of dawn a blanket curtain suddenly parted in the enemy trench. Two Argentinian soldiers struggled to get out. A pair of English paratroopers fired first. 'We didn't give them the option of getting out.' Dean Jenkins recalls simply. 'We just killed them.' Twenty years on every detail of the incident during the battle of Goose Green remains with him. 'I've never felt ashamed. I feel the whole war could, and should, have been avoided but I'm proud to have been part of it.' In 1982 he was a teenage para, serving under the legendary Colonel H. Jones who died at Goose Green, winning a VC for his one-man assault on an enemy trench. The memory of his commanding officer still makes Dean Jenkins shift uneasily in his seat, torn between loyalty and the brutal truth. 'How can you describe him? Let's say he was everything you'd expect in a paratroop CO – twelve-and-a-half feet of screaming airborne fury. If ever a man was born to die in battle it was him.'

In May 1982 Dean from Castlecroft, Wolverhampton, was Private Jenkins, a nineteen-year-old rifleman in the Second Battalion of the Parachute Regiment, 2 Para. He was 5 foot 8 inches tall and 10 stone, weighed down with 100 pounds of equipment and astonished to be off to war. 'We all thought, where the hell are the Falklands? Someone said, what are the Argies doing in northern Scotland?'

A few weeks later, at dead of night, 2 Para's landing craft sneaked into San Carlos. They expected to meet a wall of enemy fire. In the calm there was a moment of farce as hundreds of battle-ready paras failed to understand a Navy order. 'The ramp went down and this Marine said, "troops out". He said it again. It was a Navy order. No-one knew what he meant. Finally someone said "go!" and we went. It was a big anti-climax. I don't remember being frightened but we were really excited.

There was no firing. We all thought, where are they?'After a few days top brass ordered an attack on the settlement of Goose Green, held by about two thousand Argentinians. After a 'horrendous' night march of six hours Dean Jenkins and his pals crossed a wire fence. The shooting began. 'There was this sniper. He must have killed three of our lads. Every time anyone climbed over the fence he fired. It reminded me of the First World War and going over the top.'

The attack faltered. The paras were pinned down in a shallow gully. It was then that their furious colonel arrived. 'Everyone recognised H. Jones. He was tall, wearing this padded jacket, and he was shouting and moaning that we had all stopped. We were a bit aggrieved. We'd been under fire for two hours and here we were, getting the blame.'

At that moment H. Jones launched his one-man attack on an Argentinian trench. As he reached it he was killed by a burst of machine-gun fire from another trench. The debate on whether he was a hero or a fool has raged ever since. What no-one denies is that the Paras, robbed of their CO, fought like demons. 'Someone used an anti-tank rocket to destroy an enemy bunker. The Argentinians didn't seem to know what to do next. We went into our trench-clearing drill using phosphorous grenades. We literally overran them. We ran out of grenades. My partner covered me and I got to the edge of a trench. These two Argentinians were coming out . . .'He speaks quietly with not a profane word. There is no swagger, no remorse as this former Para and policeman recalls the deed. 'I didn't think about killing at the time, but afterwards we were all in this state of shock, tired and amazed that we should have survived. I can see us now after the battle, all white-eyed and white-lipped.'The Falklands War had not finished with 2 Para. With seventeen dead, and dozens wounded or suffering from trench-foot, they expected to be withdrawn. Instead they were sent to defend Bluff Cove where they witnessed the worst British disaster of the war, when the landing ship *Sir Galahad* was bombed.

'We knew the Welsh Guards were coming, but we never imagined they would come in two big ships. We watched them milling around on the deck. We knew someone would see them. We heard the air-raid warning. We knew what was going to happen. We did what we could but, honestly, the injuries . . .' *April 2002*

Burial at sea

It had been a good night for the Brits. The Falklands War was almost over. The Paras, Commandos and Guards were closing on Port Stanley. A few miles offshore the destroyer HMS *Glamorgan* was doing her bit, whamming 4.5-inch shells into Argentinian positions above the town. As dawn broke *Glamorgan* turned away. 'We had fallen out from action stations and were in the operations room,' recalls Police Constable Anton 'Aggie' Christie, in the living room of his Bilston house. 'Then we remembered we'd left our kit on the upper deck. I went to get it. I was coming back down when I felt one of our missiles, a Sea Cat, being launched. You felt the ship shudder. I just stopped and thought, what's happening? Then, a few seconds later, the Exocet hit us. There was a huge bang. They sounded action stations and I thought, that's a bit late . . .' Thirteen of his comrades died when the Exocet, fired from a launcher in Port Stanley, slammed into *Glamorgan*'s rear hanger. 'There was nothing left. The Wessex helicopter had vanished, apart from its gearbox. I saw someone lying down and realised it was a body. I knew them all. That night there was the classic burial at sea. Someone played The Last Post on a bugle, not very well, and the bodies went over the side. We were all shell-shocked.'

Until the Exocet struck, on 12 June 1982, HMS *Glamorgan*, known to all hands as 'the Glamorous Organ', had been a lucky ship. She was one of the first into action, shelling Stanley airfield on 1 May. Able Seaman Christie, just nineteen, was on the upper deck, loading the anti-radar rockets when Argentinian warplanes attacked. 'The bomb landed astern and lifted our arse-end out of the water. This aircraft suddenly shot down our starboard side and I was actually higher than the plane.'

If the enemy pilots were brilliant, some enemy soldiers were not so hot. *Glamorgan*'s crew watched in horror as an aircraft was shot down over Stanley. A few minutes later the crew got the report that the Argentinians had brought down one of their own planes. Aggie Christie recalls a 'slight cheer' at the news. But the mood changed a few days later when the first Exocet attack of the war destroyed HMS *Sheffield*. 'At first it was a game. When you're nineteen you are invincible. You can't possibly die. Even when we were getting bombed it was still a game. It was what we joined for. But after we heard that HMS *Sheffield* had been sunk, that's when it stopped being a game. We were scared some of the time but mostly we were tired. These days, you mention the Falklands War and people say, "Oh, I remember that – I was six at the time". I don't know where the years go.' *April 2002*

Horror at Fitzroy

Simon Weston has a hangover. I sympathise. 'No, it's my own fault,' he insists. 'Too much Pils last night. Still, worse things happen at sea . . .'It's a line he clearly enjoys using: a blunt, throwaway phrase in lilting Welsh tones that hits you like a boot in the guts. For at sea, off the Falklands on 10 June 1982, Simon Weston's world exploded in flames. Forty-two months on he is looking back on 1985 as 'the most fantastic year' and forward to the New Year challenge of rebuilding his life. Hideously burned, his hands a cruel parody, he talks endlessly of his good fortune, good friends, wonderful village – and mum's home-made gravy.

This year he was named one of ten Men of the Year, sharing the honours with, among others, Terry Waite, the Archbishop of Canterbury's special envoy. 'He's a hell of a nice boy, a really good bloke, know what I mean?'

I dare say Waite repays the compliment. For Simon Weston, the former Welsh Guardsman whose wrecked face speaks for all the Falklands casualties, is emerging from his ordeal as a hell of a nice bloke. 'Bitter? How can I be bitter? That Argentinian pilot only did to me what I was going to do to him or his mates. That's what war is all about.'

Simon, twenty-four, lives with his mother, Pauline, who is a district nurse, and his stepfather, Harold 'Lofty' Hatfield, in Nelson, Mid-Glamorgan. It's a neat, unpretentious community of miners and little shops, a place where people know their neighbours and Coal Board landscapers endlessly try to make slagheaps look like something else. Simon left here in 1977 to join the Welsh Guards, 'more to keep out of trouble than anything. I was a big bloke; there was always the chance I might get in a fight, hit someone and get put away. I needed discipline.'

He got it. After passing out, Guardsman 24469434 Weston served with his battalion in Kenya, Northern Ireland, Germany and Berlin. 'Of course we never expected a shooting war. Who does? Honest to God, if you knew what was around every corner, you'd never do anything.'

When the Falklands were invaded a Commando brigade was dispatched for the initial fighting. The Guards followed. 'They were going to send some other lot, some fish-and-chip bunch, but they weren't good enough. So they sent us.'

Landed at Ajax Bay, the Guards were re-embarked on *Sir Galahad* for the move to Fitzroy. They arrived and waited. Whatever the experts say now, no-one then appreciated the hazards. 'In danger? Christ, we didn't even realise we were at war. We were warm, dry and happy. We were still playing cards when it happened.'

Sir Galahad and its sister ship *Sir Tristram* were bombed by Argentinian jets. For a moment Simon loses his bounce. It's all been said. He doesn't want to talk about it. Fifty-seven died at Fitzroy. Of Simon's thirty-strong mortar platoon, twenty-two were killed outright, seven maimed and one escaped without a scratch. His best friend, Andrew 'Yorkie' Walker, was among the dead. By the normal rules of surgery Simon should have been too. Burns covered 46 per cent of his body; 40 per cent is generally regarded as fatal. But the 16-stone mortar crewman was young, fit and strong. Despite his appalling injuries he got out of the inferno unaided. The medics operated at sea to save his eyes and poured pints of saline solution into his tortured body. 'Disgusting. All I could think of was a glass of Coca-Cola with ice in.'

Back home he underwent the first of thirty-odd skin grafts. Astonishingly he was fit enough to visit home for his twenty-first birthday less than two months after the tragedy. 'The whole village put everything they could into it,' says his mother. 'He received a gold watch and champagne and so many things for the house. And all he could say was "isn't home-made gravy lovely?"' Healing takes time. With precious little skin to work with, the surgeons took grafts from his stomach and buttocks to repair his ravaged face. The operations will continue 'until me or the surgeon says enough is enough. Honest, my body looks like a patchwork quilt under this,' he says, tugging his sweatshirt. What is visible is shocking enough. 'Of course people stare and sometimes I get the rag out. If I'm upset I try to say something that will turn it round, embarrass them, not me.'

Since his injuries he has been an honoured guest of his former regiment. He laid the wreath at the Guards' Memorial; he has met his former comrades in Germany and Belgium. Becoming a celebrity – 'a minor celebrity' he insists – has made the process easier. 'I never know if they're staring because they recognise me or just because of the way I look.' *December 1985*

The sinking of HMS *Coventry*

Mel Gibson changed everything. As HMS *Coventry* sailed south from Gibraltar to the Falklands the mood was upbeat. 'At first a lot of people thought that as soon as Argentina knew we were coming there would be a negotiated settlement,' Chris Pollard recalls over a pint near his Wolverhampton home. He was a twenty-six-year-old lieutenant, the pride of an ordinary working-class family and a master gunner in charge of *Coventry*'s 4.5-inch gun and Sea Dart missiles. As the destroyer sailed south the ship's weekly film night had a profoundly disturbing effect. The movie was *Gallipoli*, the Mel Gibson film about the senseless waste of life in the First World War. 'It's a film that really brings home the hopelessness of war. Some people walked out, absolutely dead white. That film should not have been shown.'

The first days of combat hardly improved things. The ship's steering failed, her big gun kept jamming and the first long-range attacks with *Coventry*'s missiles seemed to fail. 'We were spending a lot of time sailing up and down trying to sort out the gun. I remember sitting on an ammunition box thinking, the gun doesn't work, the missiles can't hit anything and what the hell are we going to do?' On 1 May the British ships and planes attacked Port Stanley airfield. The next day the British submarine HMS *Conqueror* sank the Argentine cruiser *Belgrano*. 'We began to think, it might be easy, this.' And then, on 4 May HMS *Sheffield*, a destroyer almost identical to HMS *Coventry*, was sunk by Argentine warplanes, the first British ship to be lost. 'It had a very sobering effect. We didn't know much about what was going on, but there was suddenly this pall of smoke on the horizon.'

A few days later *Coventry* scored her first confirmed 'kill', blasting an enemy helicopter out of the sky at a range of 10 miles. 'That lifted morale.' And on 25 May a couple of attacks by enemy bombers were thwarted by Coventry and the frigate HMS *Broadsword*. As the leading aircraft were shot down a Spanish-speaking officer on *Coventry* was listening in to the Argentine pilots' radio. 'A lot of them flew around but never attacked. They were very depressed.'

But operating so close to shore, with radar which could not see over land, put the destroyer in what the former officer calls 'a suicide position'. And when the third attack came at about 4pm HMS *Coventry*'s luck ran out. 'I was standing by this sailor, only about eighteen, manning a machine-gun. His mouth was just opening and closing like a goldfish as these two Skyhawks came over. You could actually see the bombs coming down and the British markings on them. They were using British 1,000-pound bombs. I shouted "Get down!" and there was this blinding flash. The whole ship jumped. I got up and looked around. There was this big hatch and flying out of it was a mass of pipework and red rags. It must have been ten years later when I figured out that those red rags were the blokes who had been down there.'

Two bombs struck the warship, killing nineteen of the crew. As the destroyer started to sink, with her fire pumps destroyed, the crew scrambled into the sea. Chris Pollard spent twenty minutes in the water. He tried to help a Chinese laundry worker but the elderly man died of heart failure. 'At the time you feel nothing. It's all about survival. It was all very orderly. There was no panic, no screaming. All I wanted was to get as far away from the ship as possible in case she blew up.' Rescued by HMS *Broadsword*, the survivors from HMS *Coventry* were ferried to the QE2 for the voyage home. Chris Pollard believes the war could have been avoided, but is still proud to have taken part. 'I wouldn't have missed it for the world. It vindicated your professionalism. It was a chance to prove yourself. I've never understood people who say they joined the forces never thinking they would go to war. A warship is a sailing piece of death. That's what it's designed for. It's not a pleasure cruise.'

Months after the war was over he was summoned to his commanding officer to be told he had been mentioned in dispatches. The little oak leaf marking his gallantry is worn on the ribbon of his South

Atlantic medal. 'No-one ever told me what it was for, and I never asked.'
April 2002

Little tanks – a big secret

No careless talk. No cap badges to be worn. Scott Ward recalls, 'We were going to be a bit of a surprise. We were going to bend their mess tins and spoil their whole day.'

When the balloon went up in April 1982 he was a twenty-year-old tank commander in the elite cavalry regiment the Blues & Royals, with not a care in the world. 'I'd been in the Army since boy service at sixteen and I'd been in Cyprus and Northern Ireland, and now we were off on this 20,000-mile cruise. It was just like some great big adventure.'

The Task Force's 'big surprise' was a detachment of eight light Scorpion and Scimitar tanks. First ashore at the San Carlos landings, they were used throughout the fighting as mobile artillery and to carry the wounded. Because the armoured unit was so small – just twenty-four men – it got few mentions in the news reports and books about the war. But the Blues & Royals were in the thick of the action. 'The stupidest question people ask is, did you kill anyone? We did our job, and that was our job. It was a shooting war. War is all a big adventure – until you see what can happen to people.'

One of his closest friends, WO2 Danny Wight of the Scots Guards, was killed instantly by machine-gun fire. The Blues & Royals lost one tank to a landmine and two men were wounded. Scott Ward came home 'with a bit of metal in my leg' and served with the regiment for another two years before joining the police. He received two bravery awards in 2001 for trying to save a man from drowning in the river Severn at Bewdley. Chairman of the Royal British Legion in Bewdley, he returned to the Falklands on a pilgrimage in 2002, 'for the lads who didn't come back'.*April 2002*

Death of 'the Smiling Sailor'

Falklands weather. The rain hammers down like shrapnel on the conservatory roof as Rose Anslow talks about 'our beautiful boy'. His laughing face smiles back from a treasured photo on the table at her Tettenhall home. Adrian Anslow, a sailor of the Fleet Air Arm, was killed when the *Atlantic Conveyor* was attacked by Argentine warplanes in the Falklands war. He was twenty. 'They always called him the Smiling Sailor. That's how his friends remember him.'She recalls 1 April 1982 when Adrian suddenly appeared on her doorstep to announce he was being posted to an unknown destination. 'I knew instinctively, and I told him so, that he was going off to war. He said, "Don't worry, mum, I'm going to be lying under the palm trees."'

Seven weeks later there was another caller at the door. Rose Anslow remembers 'a man with a beard, looking very Royal Navy'. He broke the news that Adrian was missing. A priest called. A doctor gave her a sedative. Much of what followed is a blur. 'Adrian was simply in the wrong place at the wrong time.'

Her sailor son, a helicopter-radio specialist, was one of the first into the war zone, flying to Ascension Island by RAF Hercules to join a fleet auxiliary. After a spell on HMS *Invincible* he was part of a small naval party sent to the unarmed merchant ship *Atlantic Conveyor*. On 25 May the Argentine air force attacked what they thought was one of the two British aircraft carriers. In fact, the big blob on their radar screens was *Atlantic Conveyor*. The ship was struck and set on fire by at least one Exocet missile and sank later. Twelve men, including Adrian Anslow and the ship's skipper, Captain Ian North, were lost. Rose Anslow discovered years later that her son had been below decks at the time of the attack. She prays he died quickly.Her son was a most unlikely warrior. Adrian was a lad of strong emotions, a lover of music, fervently opposed to foxhunting and all forms of animal cruelty. Adrian's letters home as the fleet sailed to war told of his delight at seeing turtles at Ascension Island. Later he was deeply moved by the plight of his enemy. He took photographs of some Argentine prisoners of war, an encounter that made him physically sick. In one of his later letters he accepted the inevitable: 'Things are now changing, Mum. The politicians are not talking. A lot of young men are going to die and, hopefully, I won't be a hero.'

She says, 'For some reason I didn't feel he was in danger. I felt the people he was with would take good care of him. I remember hearing the news that a ship had been hit and twelve men lost. I got down on my knees and prayed for them. As far as I knew Adrian was still on *Invincible*. The next day I somehow felt uneasy. Then, that evening, the doorbell went . . .' Her voice trails away. 'Alf, my husband, has been my rock. To me, Adrian is still going on. I would hate him to look down and see his mother wasting her life. My life would be destroyed if I didn't keep setting my sights on doing things.' Like so many mothers, she is bitter about the Falklands War. She feels it should never have been fought. But she accepts this is a mother's view. Her son, her beautiful boy, would have seen things differently. Rose Anslow raises her voice defiantly over the hammering of the rain on the roof: 'Adrian had very high principles. He hated even to see birds in cages. He said everyone and everything had the right to be free. It was Adrian's war, and he went for all the right reasons.' *April 2002*

Flowers for the vanquished
The story of the flowers is enough to make your heart bleed. Brook

Hardcastle, general manager of the Falkland Islands Company, told it as he entertained us to lunch at his home in Darwin Settlement. Here, six years ago, high-explosive crashed and tracer flickered through the night sky as the Paras fought their way up the narrow neck of land towards a collection of huts called Goose Green. The scars remain. Mr Hardcastle points with pride to the bullet holes where stray shots peppered his comfortable, timber-clad house on that extraordinary night. A knocked-out Argentinian gun is on display in his garden, aimed impotently at the sapphire-blue creek where he caught our lunch, a 12-pound sea trout, a couple of days ago. Not far away is the Argentinian war cemetery where the glare from 250 white wooden crosses hurts your eyes as the sun blasts down from a deep azure sky. Some have names. But most of Galtieri's half-trained conscripts were not even given identity tags and their graves carry the motto 'An Argentinian Soldier Known Unto God'. Most of the British bodies have been brought home. Today just twenty-five remain in the neat military cemetery at Port San Carlos, overlooking the landing beaches of 'Bomb Alley' where enemy pilots showed such courage. But there is no going home for the Argentinians, not as long as Buenos Aires refuses even to discuss the matter for fear of acknowledging British sovereignty. Meanwhile, the unending saga of claim and counter-claim to these islands turns even the simplest gesture by heartbroken Argentinian families into a bureaucratic morass. To send flowers to the graves of 'Los Chicos de la Guerra' (The Children of the War), relatives must first pass them to the Brazilian embassy in Buenos Aires. The pathetic little parcels are then flown 7,000 miles to Britain, handed over to our Foreign Office, put in the diplomatic bag and flown 8,000 miles back to the Falklands. The Governor, Gordon Jewkes, dispatches them by helicopter to Mr Hardcastle who in turn takes them to the cemetery. The tiny bouquets never have names, he says, just messages in Spanish like 'My Beloved' or 'My Little Dove'; so he places them by whichever of the crosses catches his eye.

Walk northwards from Brook Hardcastle's home over the springy, gale-bent heather and you come to a small valley leading from the seashore towards the high ground. On the left of this valley is a cairn of white stones; on the right, about a hundred yards away, is a timber peg driven into the thin earth, where Lieutenant-Colonel H. Jones launched his desperately brave one-man attack. The timber peg marks the trench from which the fatal burst of gunfire came; the cairn shows where Jones fell. The colonel's grave is at Port San Carlos, a sprig of pink blossom brushing against the VC carved into the headstone. There are a dozen wreaths at the gates, plants on every grave. For the victors there is no shortage of flowers from family, comrades and islanders. For the vanquished, unknown in these distant graves, come occasional posies, wilting from the idiotic, unforgivable, 15,000-mile flight that pride and politics demand. *July 1988*

CHAPTER SIX

AFTER THE COLD WAR

A million reflections on murder

Calvary was all incense and icons. Bethlehem was traffic jams and tatty tourist trash. Some may find God there but, for me, it was as unmoving and meaningless as seeking Arthurian legend in Woolworths. And yet Israel can suddenly flay your emotions, usually when you least expect it. As when we met the children of a kibbutz on the northern border. Tiny tots singing songs and rehearsing the school play, too young to be aware that their classroom was a gas-proofed bomb shelter. Or when I talked to a nurse who tries to patch up the damage when little minds like these are torn and shattered by the sudden shriek and thump of terrorist rockets. And, of course, there was Yad Vashem, the Holocaust Museum in Jerusalem where the Nazis' efficient, businesslike, almost emotionless destruction of 6 million souls is recorded. The pictures are harrowing. Naked men and women standing at the edge of a pit full of bodies, waiting their turn to be shot. A giant of a man in a Lithuanian street, bludgeoning Jews to death with an iron bar. A street in Warsaw after the Jews had been carted off to the death camps. Pathetic bundles of clothes and suitcases left behind by the kerb.

Most poignantly of all, a tiny tot of three or four in a hand-me-down coat and outsize Andy Capp hat being led by his mother to the gas chamber. As innocent and unsuspecting as my own toddler when I lead her to the bath and I know it is hair-wash night and she does not.

There is also a new memorial, to the Children of the Holocaust. How in God's name do you commemorate 1½ million children? At Yad Vashem photographs of just a handful of the dead gaze out of the gloom, framed by four huge candles. You walk past into a vast, seemingly infinite, pitch-black place where mirror upon mirror makes endless reflections of the flickering lights. It is like moving through a galaxy, surrounded by millions of tiny sparks that twinkled briefly before being snuffed out forever at Auschwitz, Dachau and the rest.

Some hours later I arrived home in England to find my daughter standing on the kitchen dresser, face against the window, squealing with excitement. I had planned a homecoming of laughter but there is something very potent in the baby-powder softness of a tiny child, something that triggered all those images of kids in bunkers, bundles at the kerbside and a toddler in an Andy Capp hat. I held her close and cradled her head. *Jerusalem, December 1987*

Merry Christmas, Cold War is over

Of all the bars in all the gin joints in all the world, Gennadi Gerasimov had to walk into mine. The head of information at the Kremlin, anxious to escape the crush of two thousand foreign journalists in the centre of Valletta last night, booked into the cheapest room in the down-market Sa Maison Hotel on the road to Sliema and pulled up the bar stool next to mine. There are forty-one journalists staying at this hotel. The other forty are Russians. As the sole representative of the free world's media, I presented my credentials to the great man as he thoughtfully cradled a half of lager.

'Wolverhampton . . . ?'

Near Birmingham, I explained. 'Ah, Birmingham. I was there once a long time ago.' Brum did not seem to have left much of an impression.

His verdict on the Bush/Gorbachev Malta Summit? 'Very good. At last we have buried the Cold War, deep in the deepest part of the Mediterranean. Right at the bottom of the sea where it will stay from here to eternity.' His hopes for the June summit, announced yesterday? 'By the time of the Summit, START [the Strategic Arms Reduction Talks] must be finished. We want to have a real summit and that is a realistic possibility if the political will is there. Malta was a meeting of minds. It was brain-storming on what to do next in this awful world of ours. Next June we will actually sign important documents concerning nuclear and conventional weapons. Then the British official position, in support of nuclear weapons, will look outdated. These weapons have nothing to do with keeping the peace. They are just your expensive toys to play with, and some toys are dangerous. They can spoil the whole Midlands.' He grinned. 'The bigger the cuts in arms and men next June, the better. What are British troops doing in Germany? What are Soviet troops doing in Germany? They must go away, all of them. What are British troops doing in the Rhineland – why are they not in your Midlands . . . ?' *December 1989*

Gulf alchemy and the scent of war

Armageddon smells of burnt almonds. At the first whiff you must inject yourself with your Combo-pen. The Combo-pen, gentlemen. In the cold and echoing departure lounge at RAF Brize Norton the flight-sergeant held the 6-inch long automatic syringe for our inspection. We watched, fascinated, like the raw, astonished ranks of Kitchener's innocents, seventy-five years before. And, just like the boys in the poem, we had Naming of Parts. The Combo-pen. The S-10 respirator. The DKP decontamination paper and puffer pack. The rubber outer gloves ('just like Marigolds', said the sergeant), the white cotton inner gloves, looking incongruously like a conjuror's gloves, to absorb the sweat.

Today we try to remember it all, for today we are in Bahrain with the RAF strike-aircraft squadrons and well within range of the only Iraqi weapon that any of the soldiers, sailors and airmen here seem to worry about. Somewhere out there, beyond the shimmering desert horizon in the place that Saddam Hussein calls Province Nineteen and the rest of us call Kuwait, hundreds of Soviet-built Scud missiles are pointing our way.There is nothing very sophisticated about Scud. It is as primitive as its name sounds, a big rocket which is simply pointed at the infidel, launched at the appropriate elevation and lobbed in a ballistic arc. Because it is so simple, because it contains no hi-tech guidance, there is no microchip means of sending it off course. The Allied half of the Gulf is dotted with American batteries of Patriot missiles which, on exercises, regularly knock out more than 90 per cent of Scud-type targets. It is surprising how worrying 10 per cent can be. Scud can carry explosives, but in the British force area no-one is ever far from a bomb-proof shelter. The real nightmare is Scud's alternative payload, nerve gas, which arrives with no more warning than a few blue dots on the detector paper of your NBC suit or the faintest hint of burnt almonds.What was it the sergeant told us? Turn your back to the bombardment, tuck your head close to your respirator bag and pull on the face mask. Blow out hard, shouting gas, gas, gas!

And wait. And hope that none of the following symptoms begins: breathlessness, sweating, uncontrolled movements, involuntary urination or defecation. If that happens, break the seal of your Combo-pen, hold it against the fleshy part of your thigh and press the trigger. The sergeant demonstrated on a beret, the wicked inch-long needle flashing into the fabric, spitting a fine spray of atropine, a dose which, with luck, might counteract the nerve agent as it seeps into your system breaking down the muscle functions that keep your heart pumping, your lungs working.

Just as Scud is primitive, so the counter-measures seem to owe more to medieval alchemy than the twentieth century. Atropine to strengthen your heartbeat. Belladonna tablets to reduce panic. Fuller's earth to absorb the nerve-gas droplets. You look at the Combo-pen, you feel the clumsiness of your hands in two pairs of gloves. You suddenly understand what the war poet Wilfred Owen was talking about in *Dulce et Decorum Est*, his harrowing poem of a soldier drowning in chlorine because he was too slow with his gas mask. You understand 'an ecstasy of fumbling'.A corporal donned the full 'noddy suit' to demonstrate how to drink water when the air is thick with nerve gas. From the front of his respirator he uncoiled a rubber tube and clipped it into his drinking bottle. As he held the bottle high and drank it looked like some nightmarish bug-eyed moth, sipping nectar through its coiled proboscis. When the sergeant finished his hour-long briefing, part of our media party burst into spontaneous applause. They were not news hacks like the rest of us but a posse of quiet, rather thoughtful technicians and cameramen from the BBC over here to record *Songs of Praise* from the Gulf on Christmas Eve. It will be an incongruous event, a brief link between the real Britain of mortgages and foggy mornings and this other England in a sunny, sandy corner of the world where your sleeping companion is your S-10 respirator and your best pal is your Combo-pen.

Today I visited a Rapier anti-aircraft position and bumped into Corporal Simon 'Spike' Horton, from Low Hill, Wolverhampton, who has spent his time off from manning the battery in making a snowman out of chicken wire and toilet paper and finding wall space in his cramped billet for a couple of paintings from his three-year-old nephew Garth. This gift, he confesses, moved him more than he had expected. But the mood here is neither maudlin nor fearful. It is busy, purposeful and confident. It's just that now and then a child's painting may move a soldier to tears, or thoughts of Scud and the idea of almonds on the breeze make you check your Combo-pens for the twentieth time and wish you had paid more attention to what goes on back home in your own kitchen.

There are nine of us on this media trip, all male, and none of us thought to ask the most obvious question of all back at Brize Norton. It is a little worrying that, come Armageddon, none of us has the faintest idea what burnt almonds smell like. *Bahrain, December 1990*

The oldest pilot in the Gulf
The oldest RAF combat-jet pilot in the Gulf force is fifty-three-year-old Squadron Leader Dave 'Baggers' Bagshaw. The veteran who has clocked up a remarkable 9,500 flying hours on combat jets was born before the Second World War began and did his basic training on the venerable Harvard in his native Canada. He was a photo-reconnaissance pilot on Hawker Hunters during the Aden crisis in 1967 and is now back in Bahrain at what was RAF Muharraq. For all his service he has never

fired a shot in anger. As the pilot of a Jaguar low-level bomber he is rehearsing for what is expected to be a short and overwhelming air attack on Iraqi positions in Kuwait, flying daily sorties at 700mph, no more than 100ft over the Saudi desert. 'I think my reflexes are much as they used to be and my eyes may not be so good close up but at a distance they are as good as a twenty-five-year-old's. Besides, experience makes up for a lot,' said the grandfather of four.

Some of the front-line pilots have been taken aback by the sentiments in a batch of Christmas cards sent by pupils at the school near their base in East Anglia. One wrote: 'Dear Dads and Men in the Gulf, we hope you don't get shot for Christmas.' *Bahrain, December 1990*

Trauma at the 'turkey shoot'
He does not know how many men he killed. He does not want to know. All Tony Wiggan knows for sure is that the madness of the 1991 Gulf War followed him home and tore his mind apart. He became convinced his wife and father-in-law were members of the IRA trying to kill him. He found himself at the first-floor window of his house in Wolverhampton, dropping the pans, kettle and iron on to the ground below. 'At the time I thought I was being perfectly rational,' recalls the shaven-headed veteran, drawing deeply on a cigarette in his cosy living room. Above the fireplace is a souvenir, the triangular bandage issued to those Iraqi troops who had the misfortune to come up against the ferocious firepower of the Staffordshire Regiment. The Midland soldiers fought a classic battle. But there was little thought of glory as it happened.

Tony Wiggan recalls the bizarre distortion of time that goes with close combat: 'You train and train. You go through attack after attack on exercise,' says the former corporal, who commanded a section of nine soldiers and their Warrior armoured vehicle during the war. 'You come to think you're the best soldier since sliced bread, dodging about and crawling through the mud. But in the Gulf the real thing happened in pitch-black and it was raining. You couldn't see your hand in front of your face. And then it all went into this sort of slow-motion film. As I was commanding the vehicle into the attack it seemed to take for ever to get out and get around to the back. The whole section was lying down, laying fire into this trench. I knew I had to get them up. I wanted to give the order, "Charlie Fire Team – move!" but it was like we were all stuck to the ground. I suppose it only took a couple of seconds to give the order and get up, but it's like your brain's doing triple-time.' Wiggan, one of the three black section commanders in the regiment's A Company, learned something else known to every soldier in history: anyone can be brave once. Going into a second attack, to clear out a complex of four

Iraq trenches, was terror distilled. 'I couldn't believe we had to do it. We all said, God no.'

But the regiment did its job with few casualties and came safely home. With hindsight, he says, war in the Gulf probably saved his life. In barracks in Germany before the conflict, his first marriage was on the rocks and he had hit the bottle. 'It was a bad time for me. I was going into alcoholism. To be honest, the Gulf saved my liver and probably saved me. There was no alcohol of any sort in the desert, so I just had to sort myself out.'

But when he came home, having bought himself out of the Army after the war, Tony slid into a state of anxiety and irrational anger that was later diagnosed as post-traumatic stress disorder. 'It was like living with a child,' says his second wife, Gail. 'I got home to find he had cut out all the eyes from the photographs of the children.'

Her husband recalls: 'I got very anxious about seeing guns on television. I remember seeing this little lad in McDonald's playing with a toy gun. I just snapped at him. I was losing it.'

He was taken into hospital for intensive therapy, followed by out-patient sessions. But he found that writing, too, was a good way to lay the ghosts. In particular, he was haunted by what he saw in the aftermath of the American 'turkey-shoot' of Iraq troops retreating on the road towards Basra. 'You had to feel sorry for the Iraqis. The first vehicle we came across had two dead guys in it. One had a rocket straight through his head. We buried them. Then we found this third guy in the back. He'd been trapped in there for three days. The medics sorted him.'

His battlefield notes recall how the Staffords contemplated their own mortality, toyed with the idea of killing unpopular officers in battle and discovered that the greatest enemy can be your own imagination. In one plaintive passage he reflects on the despair that comes of settling into yet another trench for yet another night: 'The physical and mental strain is telling. It comes and goes like a recurring dose. Someone call time, for pity's sake.' And in one simple rhyme he tells of a soldier whose job, after months of waiting, is over in one hundred barmy, bloody hours of Desert Storm:

> The war is over, the work is done.
> Kuwait is free. Out comes the sun.
> No time to check for enemy dead.
> No time to sleep, no time for bed.
> Two long nights, a single day,
> Kuwait is free. We have earned our pay.
> *March 1997*

The first Hercules into Sarajevo

The first British mercy flight into the shattered and starving city of Sarajevo touched down dramatically at exactly 7am British time today. The pilot of the RAF Hercules, Squadron Leader Chris 'Stingray' Tingay, made a steep approach through a bank of dense clouds only 250ft above the bomb-marked runway. Although the local ceasefire has been agreed, the rattle of small arms fire and the heavy thudding of mortar rounds could be clearly heard as we landed.

'It's great to see you, good to have you here – well done, the Brits,' said Commandant Raymond Hauben of the Belgian army who is in charge of United Nations flight control at Sarajevo airport. As he spoke, 40,000 pounds of desperately needed food, baby food and medicines were speedily loaded onto white UN cargo trucks for the high-speed dash into Sarajevo. The RAF flight, codenamed Operation Cheshire, was originally planned for yesterday but was delayed until a thousand-strong Canadian infantry battalion made their way overland to secure the airport. It was a tense seventy-five-minute flight from Zagreb. The Hercules is unarmed apart from devices to jam radar and heat-seeking missiles. We sat nervously inside the Hercules, wearing flak jackets.

From the air Sarajevo, a town of 400,000 people, looked utterly deserted. No one moved through the streets. At the airport terminal, peppered with mortar holes and strewn with debris, the group of French marines peered nervously through gunslits at a wasteland of burned-out cars and shattered buildings where snipers had been seen earlier. A bullet hole inches above their positions told of an earlier near miss.

The full horror of what is happening in the Bosnian capital of Sarajevo was brought home by an army doctor, thirty-one-year-old Major Vanessa Lloyd-Davies, in charge of the airport's military hospital and a regular visitor. 'We have a nursing sister from a nearby village where they are eating grass because there is no food left. They haven't seen milk or baby food for days.'

Army medic Sergeant Geoff Newitt, a veteran of several army tours into the 'bandit country' of South Armagh said, 'Compared to Northern Ireland this is much more dangerous.'

The RAF Hercules will make a second flight into Sarajevo later today. As the international aid mission gathers pace, cargo aircraft are also arriving from America, Canada and Norway. Although today's delivery was relatively small – armed forces minister Archie Hamilton yesterday described it as 'an important drop in the ocean' – it had great symbolic significance. As senior UN official Mik Magnusson said here last night, 'If they let this flight through without shooting at it it means there's enough humanity around to send a message to the people who claim to lead these factions that there is another way out.'

Although today's mission was a success, few observers here held much long-term optimism. Mik Magnusson said he was depressed by the mutual hatred of all sides. Atrocities committed in the Balkans, he said, were worse than anything seen in Africa. 'The more cynical of us feel that a lot more blood will have to flow and be seen to flow before the international community reacts. These are poor peasant people and the world does not seem to see them dying.' *July 1992*

Major Vanessa Lloyd-Davies was found dead in 2005 aged forty-four, after suffering severe depression. The first female medical officer to the Household Cavalry, she was awarded a military MBE in 1993 for her work in Bosnia.

Too old to run away
The last line of defence yomps off into history. It is the end of the road for Dad's Army. The Home Service Force was never under any illusions about its job. As a greying HSF soldier once put it, 'We're the last line of defence because we're young enough to fight but a bit too old to run away.'

The HSF was raised in 1982 at a time when Nato chiefs were worried about the growth of Spetznaz, the Soviet equivalent of the SAS. If war came, Spetznaz units would strike far behind the front line, destroying power stations, telephone exchanges and other so-called Key Points (KPs).

The problem was that the only men available for KP defence came from the regular Army and Territorials – young, trained soldiers who would be needed at the front.

The five thousand-strong Home Service Force was the solution. Open to under fifty-fives with previous military experience, the HSF brought together a curious assortment of soldiers, sailors and airmen eager to do their bit. Prior rank counted for nothing. A retired RAF base commander might find himself serving as a private in an infantry platoon commanded by a former navy sub-lieutenant. Sceptics doubted they would be much use against Spetznaz. Yet when the Worcester-based F Company HSF was pitted against an SAS 'enemy' on one memorable exercise, the old soldiers foiled the attack, captured two SAS soldiers and were judged to have killed three others. 'I don't know whether we could have done the job,' says F Company commander, Major Jim Featherstone. 'But we were there when there was nothing else and our shooting was among the best in the country.' Now the glory days are over. This week sees the official disbandment of the Home Service Force. It is part of the 'peace dividend' process that has already led to big cuts in the regular and reserve forces and the scrapping of the Royal Observer Corps. HSF soldiers who want to stay on can transfer to their local TA units. But many have already voted with their boots. The old warriors were in it for love of their country, not money. Their annual 'bounty' was just £195. So as it dawned that the Cold War was won, the men of the HSF drifted away. From a West Midland peak of about 320, the regional HSF has dwindled to barely 200. 'It's a shame. They were a great crew and great value,' says Major Featherstone. 'The total budget for my company last year was £32,000. We had sixty or seventy men, armed and in uniform, for about the same cost as employing a single company sergeant-major in the Army. Of course, there has to be a peace dividend, but I feel very strongly that we were excellent value for money.' *June 1992*

'Bosnia Bob'

It's a restful morning for Bob Stewart, reclining on a four-poster bed at Birmingham's luxurious Swallow Hotel. I hate to spoil the moment but has he seen the *Sun*? He hasn't. 'What are the buggers saying now?'

They are saying, alongside a picture of the colonel with his Distinguished Service Order at Buckingham Palace, 'Bonking Bob Gets Yet Another Gong'. He utters a barely audible sigh. Lieutenant-Colonel Bob Stewart led the Cheshire Regiment through its historic tour of duty in Bosnia. He won the nation's admiration, in the wake of an horrific village massacre, for yelling at a carload of the local guerrillas that he didn't need their bloody permission to be where he was. And when some very silly Slavs took potshots at his convoy, it was 'Bosnia Bob' who coolly ordered his Warrior armoured vehicle to cut loose with its machine-gun. In a war where we see so much horrifying injustice and bullying, the sight of a British gun barrel equalising the odds offered a rare moment of satisfaction.

But Bosnia Bob hit the headlines for another reason. In the great tradition of English heroes, he fell for another woman. His twenty-year marriage collapsed. Bob Stewart's new book describes the confusion, frustration and sudden naked horror of the tribal war in Bosnia. As a company commander he lost eight soldiers killed in a bomb outrage during a tour of duty in Northern Ireland. But nothing touched him as much as the death, by a sniper's bullet in Gornji Vakuf, of Lance-Corporal Wayne Edwards in 1993. He helped recover the body, stood by as resuscitation failed, wept over the corpse in the medical room. 'I felt responsible. Not guilty but responsible. If you don't feel a deep sense of responsibility in situations like that, then you shouldn't bloody well be doing the job. Our mission was not to make peace. It was humanitarian, getting food and shelter through. And in the area for which we were responsible no-one died of hypothermia or starvation. I think that was pretty successful.'

How long will British troops be out there? 'How long is a piece of string? It has been going on for centuries but there must be a political solution. Perhaps people will simply get so war-weary that it stops. I never found out why it is that a farmer can have a drink with his next door neighbour, who may be of a different nationality but they are both southern Slavs, and then suddenly go off, get his gun and shoot his neighbour. I mean, how? Why? How can someone look through the cross-hairs of a telescopic sight, see a woman's head in the sight, pull the trigger and watch the head dissolve? How can they do that?' *December 1993*

Ceasefire in Derry

Clickety-click. The pictures are on the screen for barely a second yet they cannot keep up with Paddy Doherty. He's doing what he does best, promoting a city so torn by bigotry that even the name has been known to start fights. To Catholics like Doherty, one of the city's best known characters and a civil-rights veteran from the earliest days of the Troubles, this is Derry, deriving from the ancient Celtic name Doire. But the Protestants who settled here 300 years ago loved the place so much they prefixed it with London. Today it might well be called Crane City thanks to the tower cranes reshaping the skyline, and visionaries like Paddy Doherty, head of the Inner City Trust, showing off its war-wounds with a pride that borders on vanity. 'Oh, yes, the Provos blew this one up,' he says, showing a slide of the wrecked Heritage Library. 'They said there was nothing personal in it. Anyway, we just built it up again.'

The pictures flash up by the dozen: hideous piles of smoking bricks, windows burned out, like something from the Warsaw Ghetto. The IRA destroyed, the Inner City Trust rebuilt and the British taxpayer has footed most of the bill. If ever there was a case of throwing money at a problem here it is, on the banks of the Foyle in north-west Ireland. Millions are pouring into Ulster from Whitehall, Brussels and the United States, and you can't help wondering how it might be spent in less bothersome places like Walsall or Wolverhampton. Doherty is cock-a-hoop. Whatever John Major promises, however much he stresses that nothing will be done without the consent of the (Protestant) majority, Catholic triumphalism is all around. 'I think the peace will last because the British have made their minds up to get out,' says Paddy. 'It may take ten or twenty years but there is a realisation that they have to go.' But the miracle of restoring bomb-battered Derry is being done with British money. Ironic, or what? 'We're entitled to it,' Paddy Doherty says simply. He is the Irish condition distilled. In one breath he talks of a bright future and the need to heal wounds. In the next he's declaring that 'famine is part of my heritage'. And were we aware that when the Doherty clan was rounded up and sent off as enforced soldiers for the king of Sweden all the men were castrated? It happened in 1608 which, in this province of short tempers and long memories, is the day before yesterday. Twenty-five years of bloodshed have divided Derry. Once sixteen thousand Protestants lived north of the river. Today only sixteen hundred remain; the others have moved across the Foyle to the Waterside district. Here, from a vantage point on blustery Corrody Hill, Roy Arbuckle points out the distant Bogside where, in 1969, the police lost control of the riots and the British Army was drafted in. Three thousand deaths later Ulster has enjoyed six months of peace. But Protestants like Arbuckle do not trust John Major and fear that Ulster will soon be swallowed into a united Ireland. 'The Protestant community is going through a grieving process,' says Arbuckle, a community arts officer for the Waterside Trust. 'There is grief, anger, denial, rejection. People say, uh-uh, this is change that we didn't ask for and they are afraid of it. The British are on their way out, as gracefully as they arrived.' Arbuckle's boss, Waterside Trust chief executive Colm Cavanagh, is a Catholic who insists, 'We won't see a united Ireland within a hundred years.'

But in Londonderry, a worldwide symbol of Protestant rule, most people think otherwise. Six months of peace has changed everything. There are no soldiers on the streets, no checkpoints. There is nothing to distinguish Derry, confident, busy and decked with cherry trees, from any other European city, apart from this curious sense of anti-climax and uncertainty. 'These days,' confides a local reporter who cut her teeth on the Troubles, 'the news is all drug-busts, flower shows, VE Day and golden weddings. Sometimes you sort of wish for a good, old-fashioned bombing.' And in the centre of a city increasingly pinning its hopes on tourism, a local points out one of the attractions, and offers his own name for Derry/Londonderry: 'See that corner? That's where the policeman was shot just before the ceasefire. Just walked up to him and shot him dead. Just like that. This is Mad-Bastard City, this is.'

A few hours later John Major breezed into Derry, and locals demonstrated their eagerness for peace by putting twelve policemen in hospital. The mad bastards had a field day. *May 1995*

Lunch with Mr Adams
The handshake is firm, the glasses are bifocal and the smile is as wide as his credibility gap. Three floors up over South Kensington, Gerry Adams is holding court at a select luncheon paid for by his publishers. The man best known for explaining why blowing up women and children 'has to be viewed against the context of 800 years of British oppression' is

giving us the Mr Nice Guy act. He's just an ordinary married man and father, he insists. Loves cooking, laughs his way through P.G. Wodehouse novels and can often by seen on long rambles, with Pavarotti trilling through his Walkman. So tell me, how long before we see the Gerry Adams Cookery Book? He smiles broadly across the table. Elsewhere in the capital the shell-shocked survivors of last week's police raid on an IRA bomb factory are kicking their heels in prison cells. Gerry Adams is toying with chicken and pasta, sipping chilled orange, declining the wine and leaving half his chocolate mousse. Adams, according to the blurb for his new book, is 'fully committed to peace' and blaming the end of the IRA ceasefire on British feet-dragging.

His book is a bizarre read. Adams tells, apparently in all seriousness, how he heard of the ending of the IRA ceasefire seven months ago through 'rumours circulating in the media.' What? The world-famous spokesman for the IRA knew nothing of the renewed bombing campaign until a few hacks started gossiping? It is beyond belief. Over lunch, Adams insists defiantly that's exactly how it happened: 'The IRA are going to plant this huge bomb in Canary Wharf and they're going to call me up or send for me and tell me before? That's ridiculous.' Adams portrays his young self as just an ordinary Catholic lad. And then, quite suddenly in 1969, the wicked Brits arrive and start locking him up and beating him ruthlessly. For one who has taken as many beatings as Adams claims, he looks remarkably undamaged. Those celebrated wolfy teeth? Yes, they're his, he smiles, seemingly surprised to be asked. The probability is that Adams is telling the truth, as he sees it. But although he views himself as 'an ordinary individual', he stands so far away from most reasonable people, so steeped in rebel folklore (his dad was an IRA man, jailed for attempted murder), so stuck in a blinkered time-warp, that his 'truth' is a ghastly parody of the real thing. Thus, Bloody Sunday when British paras shot thirteen demonstrators in Londonderry in 1971, was 'a cold, predetermined, intentional massacre of civilians'. Yet when the terrorists staged their own Bloody Friday he insists that the IRA 'set out to cause economic damage and had sought to avoid civilian casualties'. For the record, the IRA let off twenty-one bombs in seventy-five minutes in the middle of Belfast on that terrible day, killing nine people. No-one who witnessed the security forces shovelling up the guts and body parts in Belfast bus station will ever forget it. Adams graciously concedes that the deaths were 'a matter of deep regret'.

When Gerry Adams suggests (over the cheese course) that Sinn Fein might settle, initially, for something less than the united Ireland dreamed of by every Republican since 1921, you begin to feel some pity for him. For when the legendary IRA leader Michael Collins signed the treaty with Britain and accepted a divided Ireland all those years ago he also signed his own death warrant, and was duly shot by his old IRA cronies. Does Adams worry about the assassin's bullet? For seven long seconds he says nothing. Then, 'I've already lived longer than Michael Collins.'

As we pack up, Gerry Adams beams broadly. He thinks we have got on really well.

'You were combative,' he smiles, approvingly, signing the book. Despite myself, I shake his hand again and wish him well. Better the devil you know. *September 1996*

Preparing to quit Hong Kong

The dawn came up like thunder out of China – and the Staffords attacked like lightning. The firefight at daybreak was all over in a matter of minutes. As the skies lit up with flares, machine-guns gave covering fire and the Staffordshire Regiment went into action on an anti-terrorist exercise. The squaddies stormed through two 'enemy positions' under the unblinking eye of Communist China.

Today's exercise amid the sweltering scrubland of High Peak in the far north of Hong Kong was hot, hard and sweaty. And the Staffords, over here until next February, knew their every move was being watched from observation posts in the hills just a couple of miles across the border in Communist China. The Staffords are the last but one British regiment to man the Hong Kong garrison before Britain hands the colony back to China next July. 'Sometimes you wonder why you're doing an exercise like this,' said Sergeant Brian Jackson of Willenhall, a veteran of the 1991 Gulf War. 'Then it happens for real and you know why.'

The Staffords are doing the job that British troops have done in Hong Kong since 1841, representing British sovereignty. Officially Britain is expecting a smooth handover. Privately some soldiers are not so sure. As dawn rose over High Peak, and the Black Country lads blazed away, the sun shone on the huge, defiant banners of a village of settlers who are fiercely loyal to the Chinese Nationalist Government, which was kicked out of mainland China by the Communists in 1948. The same Communist soldiers watching today's show of force by the Staffords have been monitoring these dissidents for the past forty years. No-one knows what treatment they can expect when the People's Liberation Army takes over from the British next summer. 'I reckon they'll be in for a good slapping,' said a Staffords officer grimly. *November 1996*

Anne Frank's friend

The children are younger than she expected. In Israel and across Europe Hannah Pick-Goslar is used to talking about the Holocaust to secondary-school pupils. And yet these nine- and ten-year-olds at a Black Country school listen attentively. Hands shoot up. There are some old questions, some new and unexpected ones. Like, what was Anne Frank's favourite animal? 'You know, I don't remember so much,' she chuckles in a rich Israeli accent. 'If I'd known I was going to be asked so many questions I would have asked Anne better.'

But then who could have guessed that the childhood chatter and playground games of two little girls in Holland would one day become of global interest? Anne Frank was the little Dutch girl who hid with her Jewish family in Amsterdam during the Nazi occupation. They lived in a cramped, secret apartment from 1942 to 1944 and Anne kept a daily diary. Discovered by the Nazis, the Frank family was shipped off to Nazi concentration camps. Her father was the only member of the family to survive.

Anne died of typhus in Belsen, aged fifteen, shortly before the war ended. In 1947 her father published *The Diary of Anne Frank*. It became a worldwide bestseller, chronicling the hopes and dreams of the innocent generations wiped out in the name of the Master Race. By a miracle Anne and her childhood friend, neighbour and classmate Hannah ended up in the same sector of Belsen, separated only by barbed wire. 'There was a barrier of, now what do you call them?' The old lady with a lined, sunburned face and shock of black hair struggles for the English words as we chat in the headteacher's study at Bramford primary school, Woodsetton. 'Reeds,' she says triumphantly at last. 'Like from a marsh. I could not see her through the reeds. We could only hear each other.'

Sixty years on, the image of two stick-thin teenagers sobbing in the freezing night, separated from their parents, terrified of the gas chambers and riddled with disease, is too terrible to imagine. Can these English kids comprehend the nightmare of the Holocaust? Hannah has tailored her story for little ones. 'Oh, they know all about hiding, so I tell them how Anne had to hide.' Obviously I don't tell them about the gas chambers.'

Israelis are famously blunt. She speaks her mind. Over here in England, she says, plenty of grandparents still hate the Germans. The kids can relate to that. In a recent talk in East Germany she came up against another race-memory. Those children had been briefed by their teacher the day before to be on their best behaviour. 'But this one little girl said her grandmother had told her another story, about how her grandfather had been without work and then Hitler came to power and suddenly he had work again.' The German teacher was horrified and apologetic but the truth was out. In some German homes they still believe that Hitler was a hero and that ordinary Germans knew nothing about the systematic deportation and murder of six million European Jews.

On their few stolen nights in Belsen Hannah whispered encouragement to Anne, and even managed to bundle some scraps of food together and lob them over the wire. Had they been spotted, the children would have been shot instantly. The first food was snatched away from Anne by a starving woman. The second parcel, a few days later, sailed over. 'I got it!' gasped Anne Frank. The pair agreed to meet again soon. 'Until then!' exclaimed Anne.

Those were the last words Hannah ever heard spoken by her friend. Days later Hannah was shipped to another camp. Anne and her sister Margot perished before British troops reached Belsen. All these years later Hannah Pick-Goslar is the matriarch of a big, close family in Jerusalem. Her survival, her inclusion in *The Diary of Anne Frank* and the memories she passes on, are a part of the Holocaust-memorial phenomenon that has grown quickly over the past decade. She cannot explain the sudden interest in Hitler's Final Solution. But she does not share the views of some pessimists that such a thing could happen again. Sure, there has been genocide in Africa, she says but nothing like the Holocaust. 'Not with gas chambers, not with six million. The Holocaust was all so, what is the correct word?' Organised, I suggest. 'Yes, that's it. It was so orderly, so organised, done with such efficiency. Only the Germans could do that. There is not another people like that.'

When the Nazis first invaded Holland in 1940, she recalls, life at first went on as normal. Then one day Anne Frank and Hannah went to their favourite park bench. It had a new sign: 'Forbidden to Jews'. That was how it started.

'It's a good thing to talk about it,' says the VIP as well-fed children laugh in a corridor rich with the warm, comfortable smell of school dinners. 'When you know how it starts you know how to stop it from happening again. And it cannot happen again, so long as we are strong.'
March 2001

Dambusters in the Gulf

In the deadly skies above Iraq, Squadron Leader John 'JC' Clarke sets the cross-hairs of his bomb sight on yet another of Saddam Hussein's tanks. A few seconds later the laser-guided bomb strikes. Another successful mission. 'The Army are directing us and sometimes it can take ages to find the right target,' says the RAF navigator, from Smethwick. 'But the last thing we want is any collateral damage. So, if it takes eight or ten minutes to find the right target, it is time well spent.'

In the 1991 Gulf War RAF Tornados suffered terrible losses in low-level attacks on Saddam's airfields. In this war the only Tornado lost was shot down by a US Patriot missile in an early mission. 'It was early and unexpected, and it shook us all up,' says John, whose mother Winifred, brother Michael and sisters Fern, Sonia and Dorothy still live in Smethwick. His family originally came from Jamaica. Black RAF squadron leaders are, he grins, 'definitely very rare'.

He joined the RAF in 1982 and was commissioned as an officer four years later. He serves as a navigator in a GR4 Tornado of 617 Squadron, the legendary Dambusters. Based in Lossiemouth, Scotland, he has been in the Gulf for nearly two months and has completed thirteen missions, mostly at night. Although Tornados run into occasional bursts of anti-aircraft fire, he says Gulf War II is less dangerous for the RAF crews than Gulf War I. 'Technology has come on a lot in the thirteen years since the last war. It means we can achieve our aim with slightly less risk.'

As the television images of liberated Baghdad were shown yesterday, John said he and his colleagues were elated and looking forward to the end of the war.

'But Iraq is a huge country. There could be a lot of work to be done yet.' *April 2003*

Armistice Day
He was an old soldier, alone with his thoughts on a blustery cliff-top in Normandy. Behind him, the white flecked grey of the squally English Channel. In front, the shattered remains of a mighty German bunker. Here, in a few immortal hours on 6 June 1944, the monstrous anger of the Royal Navy's big guns was unleashed on Hitler's Atlantic Wall. This bunker took a direct hit. Great chunks of concrete and shards of gun barrel still litter the meadow. As the German defences were smashed British, Canadian and American troops swarmed ashore to begin the liberation of a continent. Sixty-one years on the old soldier ran a hand thoughtfully over the cold, massive bulk of the wrecked gun breech. Had he been here before? As soon as I asked the question, it all came pouring out. Old soldiers who never breathe a word to their families about the demeaning, disgusting, terrifying and glorious business of warfare sometimes open up to inquisitive strangers.

His name was Bryan Johnson but everyone called him Dogger. Back in 1944 he was a twenty-three-year-old tank driver, coming ashore with the 5th Royal Tank Regiment in the dangerous hours after D-Day. The narrow lanes of the Normandy Bocage countryside were a nightmare for the tanks. Endless ambushes wore down the nerves. Dogger's luck held for more than a month. On 18 July hundreds of British tanks moved forward in the assault codenamed Goodwood. In the open fields his comrades were picked off like flies by the Germans' formidable 88mm guns. 'It was just slaughter. We lost 400 tanks that day. My co-driver was killed.' By rights Dogger should have died, too. But by one of those miracles of combat he was adjusting his seat in the tank and suddenly dropped a few inches. At that moment the shell struck. His co-driver, Aubrey Garrett, was mortally wounded. Aubrey took some time to die. Dogger did what he could. 'His brains were all over the place. It's the only time I have ever administered morphine to a man as he was dying.' As we stood on the clifftop Dogger reflected on the unfairness of it all. In one flash of high explosive Aubrey died but Dogger got another sixty-odd years. Dogger and his mates won the war, came home and kept their memories to themselves. On Armistice Day these survivors stand in silence with memories too terrible to comprehend. And if they shed a tear is it any wonder? *November 2005*

A death in Afghanistan
His name was Gordon but, because he was always on the plump side, everyone in the Squadron called him Twiggy. We laid him to rest a few days ago. It has been a sad time for my old Territorial Army unit, 67 (the Queen's Own Warwickshire and Worcestershire Yeomanry) Signal Squadron. Exactly a week before Twiggy's funeral the lads paid their last respects to Joe Whittaker, just twenty and killed by a landmine while serving in Afghanistan. Sergeant Gordon 'Twiggy' Aylett died of cancer. He was sixty-three.

The contrast between the old TA and the new has never been sharper. My generation were Cold War warriors, little khaki cogs in the nuclear-tipped machine known as Mutually Assured Destruction. If Britain had been threatened by war we would have been mobilised, just as the Territorials were in two world wars, and sent to do or die. Today the old notion of calling up entire TA units has passed. Instead, individual soldiers are invited to volunteer for Iraq or Afghanistan.Joe Whittaker, a bright, much-loved lad, went for it, and paid the ultimate price. After serving two years with 67 Squadron he transferred to the Parachute Regiment. On 24 June 2008 he stepped out of his vehicle in Helmand Province and was blown up by a landmine.

My generation trained for the ultimate war yet never fired a shot in anger. Joe perished in a nasty little scrap which no-one could have predicted. None of us will know how we would have faced combat, but I know Twiggy would have been a good soldier. In civilian life he was a carpenter and builder, a gentle family man with a shed full of widgets and tools. But on the ranges he was the best shot I ever knew, a solid, steady gun platform who would take infinite patience as he attempted to keyhole each bullet hole into the one before. He was a great procurer, too. As a young officer I lived in mortal dread of audits, when a team of grim-faced inspectors crawled over my troop stores to ensure not a single radio valve or gun-cleaning kit was missing. Come the day, by some miracle (and you never asked too many questions), every item on the inventory was in its place. Twiggy had been busy.

He served for more than twenty years and was the sort of reliable, endlessly cheerful NCO who has always held the British Army, both Regular and TA together. He died too young. But he lived to see the centenary of the Territorial Army and at least he was spared the dismal prospect of its final act. Under the demands of Iraq and Afghanistan the TA shrank to barely twenty thousand. It may be wound up. If that happens, Britain's unique citizen army, 100 years old in 2008, will pass into history. The rich, life-enhancing comradeship of weekend warriors will go with it, and so will Britain's priceless ability, described in this book, to reinforce its regular armed forces speedily if some great calamity faces us, as happened in 1914 and 1939.

How bizarre it all is. When the Berlin Wall came down in 1989 we quietly celebrated the end of the Cold War. We looked forward to something politicians called the 'peace dividend'. Instead, the madness of 9/11, Iraq and Afghanistan took over and today old soldiers and young soldiers are being buried within days of each other. And so this book, which opened with memories of General Gordon at Khartoum, ends as it began, with British soldiers fighting and dying in dusty, far-off lands we barely understand. *September 2008.*

Lightning Source UK Ltd.
Milton Keynes UK
12 October 2010

161179UK00001B/57/P